the MOTOR CAR

the
MOTOR CAR
an illustrated international history
by David Burgess Wise

Special photography by J. Spencer Smith

G. P. PUTNAM'S SONS New York

Orbis Publishing is indebted to the following for allowing their cars to be photographed: Briggs Cunningham Automotive Museum; Château de Grandson, Switzerland; Cheddar Motor Museum, England; Coventry Motor Museum, England; Fiat Centro Storico, Italy; Peter Hampton, England; Dr John Mills, England; National Motor Museum, England; Peugeot Collection, France; Saab-Scania, Sweden; Franco Sbarro, Switzerland; E. Schmidt, Switzerland; Hank Schumaker, England; Science Museum, England; Skokloster Museum, Sweden; Stratford Motor Museum, England; Ben Wright, England.

Picture acknowledgements
Alfa Romeo: 305b – American Motors: 323a – Audi: 305a – Autocar: 149a, 155, 158 – Automobile Museum, Turin: 54b, 54–5a & b, 55, 59a – Bayer Armee Museum: 160 – Belli: 60 – Boschetti: 43a & b – N. Bruce: 168, 260 – Bundesarchiv: 161a – C. Burgess Wise: 2–3, 180, 240a & b – L.J. Caddell/ Orbis: vii, 22–23, 309c, 316a & b, 317a & b, 319, 320a, 321a, 324a – Chrysler: 304a – Citroën: 199b, 280, 318–9, 323b – D. Copsey/Orbis: 76, 91a & b – M. Decet: 314b – De Gregorio: 3b – Ford: 83, 98a, 152a–c, 153, 241, 262a & b, 266–7b, 268–9, 270, 275, 286, 297b, 298a, 304b, 314c, 327b – G. Goddard: 294 – Hull Museum: 94–5b – Leyland: 296, 300a, 309b, 312, 324b – K. Ludvigsen: 326a – Mansell Collection: 1, 5, 7b, 14, 16–17, 18–19, 20, 21a & b, 24–5, 26–7, 27, 30–31, 36a, 45, 58a, 59c, 70a & b, 73c, 74a, 75a & b, 77, 78a, 83b, 94–5a, 106 – Mary Evans Picture Library: 2, 4a & b, 7a, 8c, 9, 15b, 22, 29, 30, 32–3, 34, 35b, 37, 40b, 42, 42–3, 48–9, 52a & b, 73a, 88a & b – Mercedes-Benz: 48a & b, 49b, 50–51, 53b, 61, 62, 62–3, 65, 307b – Motor: 308 – Musée National des Techniques: 6, 40a, 53a, 56–7 – National Motor Museum: v, 8d, 10–11, 15a, 47b & c, 72, 76–7, 78b, 82–3, 84, 84–5, 89, 91c, 93, 108, 114a, 115a, 118–9a, 121, 122–3, 126–7, 137b, 186–7, 199a, 215, 217, 220, 225, 245a, 274, 281, 282, 292, 295a, 297c – J. Neal East: 216–7, 226, 227 – NSU: 306, 326b – Orbis: 8a, 10a, 11a & b, 12, 13a & b, 35a, 39a & b, 41, 74b – Quattroruote: 3a, 36b–d, 44a–c, 46–7 – Radio Times Hulton Picture Library: 190–91, 191a & b – Renault: 327a – Robert Hunt Picture Library: 148a & b, 149b, 150–51, 154–5, 162–3, 267, 268 – Rolls-Royce: 112–3, 310b, 316–7 – Saab: 328a–c – Toyota: 321b – Volkswagen: 247a, 307a – Volvo: 309a – I. Ward/Orbis: 18, 26, 320b – N. Wright/Orbis: vi, viii, 170–71, 202–3, 210, 210–11, 211a & b, 222–3, 223, 228–9, 231, 256, 276–7, 287, 290–91, 299 – all other photographs were taken specially for Orbis by J. Spencer Smith
Front cover photograph by L. J. Cadell/Orbis and National Motor Museum
Back cover photograph by J. Spencer Smith/Orbis

Printed in Great Britain by Colorgraphic Ltd, Leicester
Library of Congress Catalog Card Number: 77-2500
SBN: 399-12025-4

Contents

Foreword
by Lord Montagu of Beaulieu

Top: motoring in the early days was very much an open-air hobby, as represented by this 1898 Daimler (Coventry Museum, England)

Above: cars like this elegant Cord 81.2 of 1936 made America the centre of grandiose styling of the motor car

Right: Lord Montagu of Beaulieu with a magnificent 4½-litre Bentley

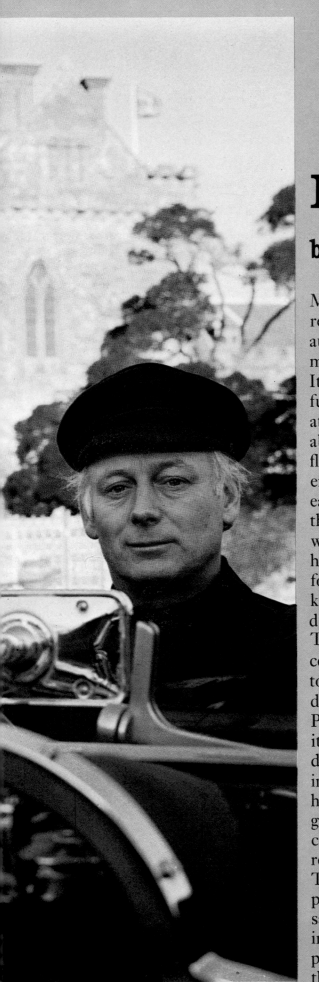

Foreword

by Lord Montagu of Beaulieu

Motoring history is now entirely respectable, and a recognised branch of scholarship. The literature of the automobile has become an essential concomitant of the museum, the rally and the motor race.

It has been my good fortune to be associated with the furtherance of this branch of the art. From earliest days we at Beaulieu recognised that people like to know more about the cars they drive or even observe upon the museum floor. They are fascinated by the pioneers whose faith enabled the motor car to overcome the prejudices of the early vehicles, by the designers who strove to conquer their imperfections, and by the engineers who made roads worthy of the new locomotion. Automobile competitions have attracted a following surpassed perhaps only by football. Restorers of barn-weathered wrecks need to know the correct equipment with which to refurbish their discoveries, be this a carburettor or merely a colour scheme. To this end we have sought to create one of the finest centres of specialist documentation in the world, and also to produce or sponsor serious historical works. By so doing we also contribute to such books as the present one. Perhaps the greatest attraction of motoring history is that it is still being made. Everyone knows Henry Ford's damnatory dictum 'History is bunk' – perhaps excusable in the case of one who was himself too busy making history – but even the great American industrialist has given us the magnificent Greenfield Village museum complex in the United States. In any case it is now recognised that history does not stop at 1914, or even 1939. The story is gaining in scope as the automobile's protagonists face new hurdles – congestion, emission, safety and now the energy crisis, allied to a worldwide inflation that once again highlights the need for a new people's car to follow in the wheeltracks of the Model T, the Volkswagen and the Mini.

It is, of course, impossible to break entirely new ground in any written history, be it of motoring or of any other subject. *The Motor Car* has, however, avoided every pitfall that attends the unwary historian. There is often a tendency for authors to skip smartly through the periods that interest them least. This David Burgess Wise has not done, giving a fair share of the text both to the primordial (on which nothing new remains to say) and to the modern.

Better still, he has used illustrations and captions to add a third dimension that will appeal to the more selective and knowledgeable reader, and here, the book scores an unqualified 'alpha'. Immense pains have been taken, not only to eliminate hackneyed shots but to seek out illustrations of less obvious cars from less obvious places. Where lesser works have contented themselves with easily available, if not very original, photographic material, the publishers of *The Motor Car* have gone out to look for vehicles rather than for prints and transparencies.

Above left: a car which ably illustrated how far motoring had progressed in a technical sense by the 1970s was the Citroën SM with its hydro-pneumatic steering and suspension

Below: on performance, this Barker-bodied Model J Duesenberg of 1929 is not far behind the space-age Citroën although its speed was achieved more with brute force than finesse

Montagu of Beaulieu

CHAPTER 1

The Horseless Carriage

'There is in this city', wrote the Parisian Gui Patin in January 1645, 'a certain Englishman, son of a Frenchman, who proposes to construct coaches which will go from Paris to Fontainebleau and return within the same day, without horses, by means of wonderful springs . . . If this plan succeeds, it will save both hay and oats . . .'

So it was, over three hundred years ago, that the first horseless carriages crept onto the scene, not with the hiss of steam or the bark of internal combustion, but with the whir of clockwork and the rumbling of crude wooden gearing like that of a mill; not that such machines were anything but elaborate and costly toys. The invention of the anonymous Franglais ran strongly, it is recorded, on trial within the confines of the Temple in Paris, but the wages of the two strong-arm men who turned the handles to wind up those 'wonderful springs' were found to exceed the cost of horses, hay and oats by an unacceptably excessive degree.

The ingenious inventors persisted, however. In 1649, Hans Hautsch of Nuremberg built an elaborate triumphal carriage with the forward end in the shape of a sea monster. This was, it seems, the fifth carriage built by Hautsch, who was born in 1595 and died in 1670, and was the most celebrated mechanic in that city of clockmakers; his inventions were powered by springs and could travel at two thousand paces an hour. He even established an export trade, selling one carriage to Prince Charles-Gustav of Sweden, for 500 rixdollars, and another to the King of Denmark. The latter machine, built in 1663, 'could go forward, backwards and turn without the aid of horses, and cover 3000 measured paces in an hour, solely by the action of cranks turned by two children concealed in the body of the carriage, which make the rear wheels revolve, and he who is within a rod which turns the front of the carriage, where are attached two little wheels to point at the desired place'.

Another technological dead-end which was being avidly pursued at that period was the sail-powered carriage, pioneered by Dutchman Simon Stevin, who in 1600 constructed a vast two-masted 'flying chariot' for the Prince Maurice of Orange-Nassau, which was mentioned in Laurence Sterne's rambling novel *Tristram Shandy* and was thus, if only peripherally, the first horseless vehicle to be featured in literature.

In 1648, one Bishop Wilkins proposed a windmill-driven carriage, while in 1714 a French inventor named Du Quet patented two extremely curious wind-powered carriages, one using a two-bladed sail to work little legs which pushed the vehicle along, while the other had a twelve-bladed fan operating racks geared to the wheel hubs. Du Quet's patent drawings also included the first-ever suggestion for wheels pivoting on stub-axles instead of the centrally pivoted cart-axle, fine when a vehicle was being drawn by horses, but liable to cause it to tip over when it was driving itself along.

Even in the nineteenth century, experimenters were still building sail-driven vehicles, and seemed to have virtually overcome the problem of running against

Below: the earliest attempts at horseless transport included many wind-driven vehicles. This is French inventor Du Quet's second patent, which appeared at the Academy of Sciences in 1714. The twelve-bladed fan operated racks geared to the hubs

an opposing wind, so that the carriage could be used on roads rather than on beaches (like their lineal descendants, the sand-yachts of today).

In 1826 and 1827, the *Charvolant* of the Englishman George Pocock ran successfully at speeds of 15–20mph, drawn by a train of steerable kites. One useful side-effect of this method of propulsion was that the lift of the kites lessened the effective unsprung weight of the carriage, and made it extremely smooth-running. One evening, Pocock had halted in front of an inn on the Bath Road. 'Just as we were preparing to depart, the London stage came by; it was almost fifteen minutes ahead when the *Charvolant* set out, but after a run of four miles, the *Charvolant* was alongside it; its efforts were fruitless, and after a run of ten miles, we entered Marlborough twenty-five minutes ahead of the stage-coach.'

A Frenchman named Hacquet was seen in the streets of Paris in 1834 with a three-masted carriage named *l'Eolienne*, which had a mainmast forty feet high. On 18 September it gave a public demonstration. 'Leaving the Ecole Militaire with a south-westerly wind, it crossed the Pont d'Iena, followed the Quais with the same wind, finally halting in the Place Louis-XV. The most curious features of this experience were having weathered a violent squall and having taken the rise of the Pont Louis-XV against what was virtually a head-wind.'

However, by that time the wind wagon had become an obsolete curiosity; for many years, inventors had been turning their attention to less fickle forms of propulsion. As far back as the 1680s, the Jesuit priest Ferdinand Verbiest had built a little steam-powered model carriage while he was on missionary duty in China. In 1685, he wrote a treatise in Latin, *Astronomia Europaea*, which was published two years later. In it he wrote: 'About three years ago, while I was making some researches into the power of the aeolipyle (a small boiler), I constructed a little chariot about two feet in length, in the middle of which I placed a container full of glowing embers, and then above this an aeolipyle. On the axle of the front wheels, there was a ring of bronze with teeth engaging in wheels linked to a shaft carrying four blades, on which the jet of the aeolipyle impinged. By means of a tiller linked to the rear axle, which could pivot, the machine could be made to describe a circle'.

In 1690, Denis Papin, the Frenchman who invented the pressure cooker, proposed an 'atmospheric machine' driven by a piston acting on a ratchet wheel, then in 1698 he built a little model steam carriage. 'As I believe that this innovation can be used with advantage for other ends than raising water, I made a model of a little chariot which moved itself by means of this force, and it achieved all that I had anticipated . . . I believe that the inequalities and twistings of the main roads will make it very difficult to develop this invention for use in land carriages.'

At the beginning of the 18th century, Father Grimaldi, another Jesuit on the China Mission, is said to have followed in the wheeltracks of Father Verbiest, building a little model steam carriage propelled by an aeolipyle in an attempt to convert the Chinese Emperor, Kang Hi, to Christianity. The machine ran successfully; whether the proselytisation of Kang Hi was as successful is not recorded.

The first British inventors to move into the as yet ethereal realms of self-propelled vehicle design were two optimists named Ramsey and Wildgoose, who in 1618 took out a gloriously vague patent for 'newe, apte, or compendious formes or kinds of engines or instruments to plough grounds without horse or oxen; and to make boates for the carriage of burthens and passengers runn upon the water as swifte as in calmes, and more safe in stormes, than boates full sayled in great winnes'.

All this, mark you, without specifying any precise form of motive power. Nor was Ramsay any more specific when he subsequently patented: 'a farre more easie and better waye for soweing of corne and grayne, and alsoe for the carrying of coaches, carts, drayes, and other things goeing on wheels, than ever yet was used and discovered'.

In 1680, Sir Isaac Newton, who had been laughed to scorn when he prophesied that one day men would be able to travel at fifty miles an hour, described

2

Abriß vom Triumphwagen

den von einem Meister deß Circkelschmidt Handwercks/ist so groß al geht/wie er da vor Augen sieht/vnd bedarff keiner Vorspannung wa der lincken Hand ein Flacinkopff inhanden/damit kan er den Wagen Thal/wie er dann vnterschiedlich mal/ist die Vestung zu Nürnberg h vmb/vnd geht solcher Wagen in einer Stund 2 tausent Schritt/ m alles von vhrwerck gemacht/wird alles mit der lincken Hand regiert hen/die Augen verwenden/der Meerdrach kan Wasser/Bier/We Dargegen kan er allerley wolriechende Wasser geben/als zumm Posaunen auffheben vnd blasen/vnd ist solcher Wagen alle Sontag vnd gilt ein schlechter P

Far left: the inventor of the pressure cooker, Denis Papin, produced in 1698 a model steam car, although he believed at the time that the idea would not work on full-size 'land carriages'

Left: long before it was generally thought to be needed, Leonardo da Vinci had already produced a differential drive system. In fact, even when motor vehicles had reached quite an advanced stage, the use of a device to distribute dissimilar amounts of torque to each wheel was still thought to be unnecessary

Below: a different and probably less efficient way of using wind power than that proposed by Stevin is seen on this model of Valturio's carriage of 1472. Even at this early time, it was realised that there was a future in vehicles powered by means other than oxen or horses

Left: the elaborate *Triumphwagen*, built by the famed Nuremberg mechanic Hans Hautsch in 1649. The vehicle, with a front shaped like a sea monster, could cover 2000 paces in an hour, powered by its clockwork mechanism. Perhaps greater mileage could have been attained had there not been so much decoration on the body to weigh the machine down

a 'scientific toy' in the shape of a little boiler mounted on wheels and propelled solely by the force of the jet of steam issuing from a nozzle leading backwards from the boiler, a concept unlikely to succeed in model form and doomed to failure in full-scale.

By the mid eighteenth century, the steam engine had been developed to the extent that it could be built sufficiently small and sufficiently powerful to be usefully installed in a road carriage, and such a vehicle was proposed in 1759 by one Doctor Robinson, a student at Glasgow University, who subsequently became Professor of Natural Philosophy at Edinburgh University. Robinson mentioned his scheme to his friend James Watt, but soon afterwards went abroad, and proceeded no further with his invention.

Six years later, three distinguished scientists began a correspondence regarding the use of steam as a motive power. It seems that one of them, Matthew Boulton of Birmingham (who became partner to James Watt), had built a little steam engine, and had sent it to Benjamin Franklin, who was then the London agent for the United Provinces of America. Franklin, his mind already abuzz with political matters, dismissed the invention with the throwaway remark that: 'It was believed to be practicable to employ it as a means of locomotion'.

This caught the imagination of the third member of the group, Doctor Erasmus Darwin, a poet as well as a physician, who wrote to Boulton: 'As I was riding home yesterday, I considered the scheme of the fiery chariot, and the longer I considered this favourite idea, the more practicable it appeared to me. I shall lay my thoughts before you, crude and undigested as they appeared to me . . . and as I am quite made of the scheme, I hope you will not shew this paper to anyone. These things are required: (1) a rotary motion, (2) easily altering its direction to any other direction, (3) to be accelerated, retarded, destroyed, revived, instantly and easily, (4) the bulk the weight, the expense of the machine to be as small as possible in regard to its weight'.

Darwin then went on to describe a rather crude device mounted on three or four wheels, driven by a two-cylinder Newcomen engine of the type used for pumping water out of mines. 'And if this answers in practice as it does in theory,' concluded the good doctor, ignoring the fact that the Newcomen engine, in which the pistons were sucked down by the condensation of steam in the cylinders creating a partial vacuum, was a bulky, slothful, inefficient device, quite unsuited to powering a road vehicle, 'the machine could not fail of success.'

It could, though, and it did. Boulton was unwilling to become a partner in Darwin's enterprise, and the scheme was allowed to lapse, although Darwin did turn the experience to some account by composing a poem which started: 'Soon shall they force, gigantic steam, afar haul the slow barge or urge the rapid car . . .' It was left to his grandson, Charles, to establish the fame of the family name.

In 1769, came the most fanciful scheme yet proposed. One Francis Moore, a rich linen draper, announced that he had obtained a Royal Patent for 'a new machine made of wood, iron, brass, copper or other metals, and constructed upon peculiar principles, and capable of being wrought or put in motion by fire, water or air, without being drawn by horses, or any other beast or cattle; and which machines, or engines, upon repeated trials, he has discovered would be very useful in agriculture, carriage of persons or goods, either in coaches, chariots, chaises, carts, wagons, or other conveyances, and likewise in navigation, by causing ships, boats, barges, and other vessels to move, sail or proceed, with more swiftness or despatch'. So confident in the omnipotence of this new motive power was the inventor that he had not only disposed of all his horses, but had also persuaded many of his friends to do the same.

James Watt dismissed the news of Moore's invention with scorn: 'If linen draper Moore does not use my engine to drive his chaises, he cannot drive them by steam. If he does I will stop him. I suppose by the rapidity of his progress and puffing, he is too volatile to be dangerous'.

However, the same year that Moore proposed his 'new machine', the first full-sized steam carriage made its appearance in Paris, the work of a French military engineer named Nicolas Joseph Cugnot, born at Void, in Lorraine, in

Left: Erasmus Darwin (the grandfather of Charles, whose biological theories were to provoke such a furore a half-century later), *above*, and Matthew Boulton, *below*, who together with Benjamin Franklin corresponded on the use of steam as a motive power. Boulton had, in fact, built a model steam engine and had shown it to Franklin. Although Franklin was indifferent about the whole idea, Darwin was most impressed. Darwin's idea centred around using a two-cylinder Newcomen engine, as utilised in mining-pump engines. This, however, was not to Boulton's thinking, so it was left up to the poet Erasmus to wax lyrical about the prospects of the steam engine

Below: in being mentioned in *Tristram Shandy*, by Laurence Sterne, this massive land yacht became the first horseless vehicle featured in literature. It was built in Scheveningen in 1600 by Dutchman Simon Steven, for Prince Maurice of Orange-Nassau

1729. As a young man, Cugnot lived in Germany, where he entered the service of the Emperor. He was, it seems, posted to Brussels in the early 1760s and, according to tradition, built a model steam carriage there in 1763.

It was in 1769, though, that Cugnot was enabled to realise his brainchild in full scale, as L-N Rolland, Commissaire-General of Artillery, recalled in a report published on the 4th Pluviose in Year VIII of the French Revolution (1801): 'In 1769 (old style), Planta, a Swiss officer, proposed a number of inventions to Minister Choiseul. Among these was a carriage moved by steam.

'General de Gribeauval, having been called in to examine the prospectus of this invention, recalled that a certain Cugnot, who had worked as an engineer in foreign parts, and author of a work entitled *Fortification of the Countryside*, was then engaged in the construction of a similar machine in Paris; the Swiss officer was instructed to make an examination of it. He found it in all ways preferable to his invention, and Minister Choiseul authorised Cugnot to complete at the State's expense that which he had begun on a small scale.

'In the presence of General Gribeauval and many other spectators, and carrying four persons, it ran on the level, and I have confirmed that it could have covered 1800 to 2000 *toises* (2.1800–2.4222 miles) an hour if it had been run without interruption.' However, the capacity of the boiler had not been accurately enough proportioned to that of the pumps, and it could only run for twelve to fifteen minutes at a time, and then had to stand for nearly as long so that the steam could build up to its original pressure; besides, the furnace being badly made allowed the heat to escape and the boiler seemed hardly strong enough to contain the full strength of the steam.

This trial having shown that a full-scale carriage would actually work, engineer Cugnot was ordered to build another, this time capable of carrying a load of 8 to 10 *milliers* (about 4 tons) at a steady speed of around 1800 *toises* per

hour; it was completed at the end of 1770, at a cost of 22,000 livres.

Cugnot's second carriage had twin cylinders (cast in the arsenal at Strasbourg and brought from there with all possible speed to Mazurier, quartermaster of the Paris Arsenal, where the *fardier* was being built). Steam was admitted to the cylinders through a rocking valve, the pistons going up and down alternately and turning ratchets either side of the single front wheel. Ahead of this wheel was supported the massive boiler, which could only (and then with difficulty) be replenished when the vehicle was at a standstill. This whole clumsy mass turned with the front wheel; steering was through handlebars which operated a geared-down pinion acting on a curved rack. It must have been a near super-human operation, as the entire power pack was supported only by one in-substantial-looking kingpin, which gave the driver a lot of work.

As the Cugnot carriage was intended as an artillery tractor, there was no superstructure on the rear part of its wooden chassis. Without a load to keep the back wheels on the ground, the *fardier* must have been terrifyingly unstable. Nevertheless, a letter written on 20 November 1770 recorded '. . . a fire engine, for the transport of carriages and, especially, artillery, has been developed to the point where, last Tuesday, this machine has pulled a load of 5 *milliers* while simultaneously carrying a cannon of around the same weight, covering five quarters of a league in an hour. The same machine can climb the rockiest heights and overcome all irregularities of the terrain'.

The last comments were, it seems, mere embroidery for, although it seems likely that the Cugnot did run under its own power, it was manifestly not a success. Cugnot's obituary, published in *Le Moniteur* of 6 October 1804, stated that the carriage was 'built in the Arsenal and put to the test. The excessive violence of its movements prevented its being steered and, as early as its first trial, a piece of wall which happened to get in its way was knocked down. That's what prevented it being put into service'.

Cugnot's *fardier*, showing a ratchet from the cylinders (one either side) that turned the front wheel. Interestingly, the latest French Citroëns use a similar layout to that of the Cugnot wagon, with the engine mounted forward of the driven front wheels. This claimant to the distinction of being the original Cugnot is in the Conservatoire des Arts et Métiers in Paris, although some authorities believe it to be a replica

Right: early trials of Cugnot's *fardier* revealed shortcomings in its controllability, graphically illustrated by this scene from its first trials in which it demolished part of a wall

Below: the kite-powered Charvolant, a flight of fancy invented by George Pocock and tested in England in 1826

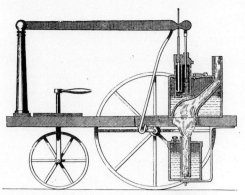

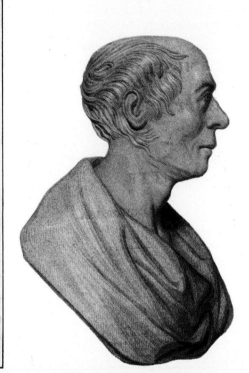

Left and below left: this model steam engine was built *circa* 1784 by William Murdock of Redruth, Cornwall. The little vehicle, standing just over one foot in height, was tested by its designer. 'The night was dark, and he alone sallied out with his engine, lighted the fire, a lamp under the boiler, and off started the locomotive, with the inventor in full chase after it. Shortly after he heard distant despair-like shouting; it was too dark to perceive objects, but he soon found that the cries for assistance proceeded from the worthy pastor, who, going into town on business, was met on this lonely road by the fiery monster, whom he subsequently declared he took for the Evil One *in propria persona*'

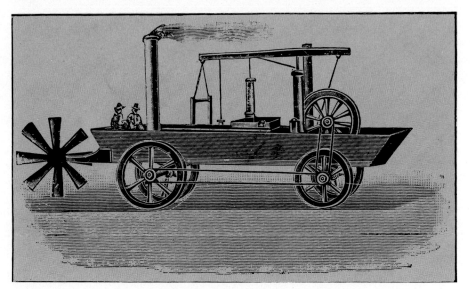

Right: Oliver Evans, in Philadelphia, built this twenty-ton amphibian, *Orukter Amphibolos*, in 1805. It was powered by a twin-cylinder grasshopper beam engine and made what is generally accepted as the first journey by a steam-powered vehicle on the American continent.

Above left and left: William Symington and his model steam coach of 1786. The state of the roads in his native Scotland at that time meant that such a vehicle in full size would not be practical. Thereafter, he concentrated on the use of steam to propel boats

It was preserved, though. It survived the French Revolution and was acquired for the Conservatoire des Arts et Métiers in 1799. Put on display in 1801, it has remained the star exhibit of this museum of technology ever since. Also surviving is a little model steam carriage built around 1784 by the Englishman William Murdock, who was in charge of the construction of Boulton & Watt beam engines in the Cornish mines around Redruth. It was a far more practicable design than that of Cugnot, but unfortunately lacked the massive Government backing which had enabled the French inventor to realise his project as a full-size machine. Indeed, it seems that James Watt was more than a little jealous of his assistant's model carriages, and sought to divert him from such projects, although on several occasions the models made successful test runs. In September 1786, Boulton wrote to Watt that Murdock had caused his little steam carriage to run for a mile or two (doubtless in a circle!) in the drawing room of a mutual friend, carrying as ballast the fire-tongs, poker and coal-shovel.

Several other inventors were also working on the development of steam carriages around the same time; they, too, got no further than the model stage. For example, in Edinburgh in 1786, William Symington proposed a curious steam berline, but the dreadful state of the Scottish roads at that period caused him to turn his attention to the more immediate problems of applying steam power to the propulsion of boats – in 1788, he built the first British steamboat to the order of Patrick Miller of Dalswinton, Dumfriesshire, which on its initial trial carried the poet Robert Burns among its passengers.

In 1788, Nathan Read, of Massachusetts, built a model steam carriage of curious design, while around the same time one Doctor Apollos Kinsley is reported to have driven a steam carriage through the streets of Hartford, Connecticut . . . although it has been recorded that it is doubtful whether the story has much basis in fact.

The true pioneer of steam propulsion in America – although his activities in other aspects of engineering outweighed his achievements in vehicle manufacture – was Oliver Evans, born in Newport, Delaware, in 1755. Today, Evans is chiefly remembered as a pioneer of automation in manufacturing processes, but as a young man he devised a high-pressure steam engine and considered its application to land carriages.

He petitioned the Legislation of Delaware in 1786 for an exclusive licence to use his automatic mill machinery and to build and use steam wagons. The Board granted the privileges he prayed for, respecting the improvements in flour-milling machinery, but they quietly ignored his steam carriage schemes altogether . . . they believed him to be somewhat deranged.

A similar request was placed before the Legislature of Maryland, and here Evans's case was pleaded by a friend on the committee, who stated that 'no one in the world had thought of moving carriages by steam, and by granting the request, no one could be injured, and there was a prospect of something useful

Trevithick and Vivian's second carriage was a massive piece of equipment with the boiler at the rear. Built in 1803, it proved quite successful, making many journeys through London and the provinces. The Felton body, mounted above the engine, could hold eight or nine people. The machine was so reliable that Vivian would take the carriage out on his own without Trevithick. It was while Vivian was driving, however, at a speed in excess of 9 mph, that a mishap occurred. The machine was running so happily that he and Trevithick joked of carrying on towards Cornwall. Vivian's concentration waned and he steered into garden fencing in City Road.

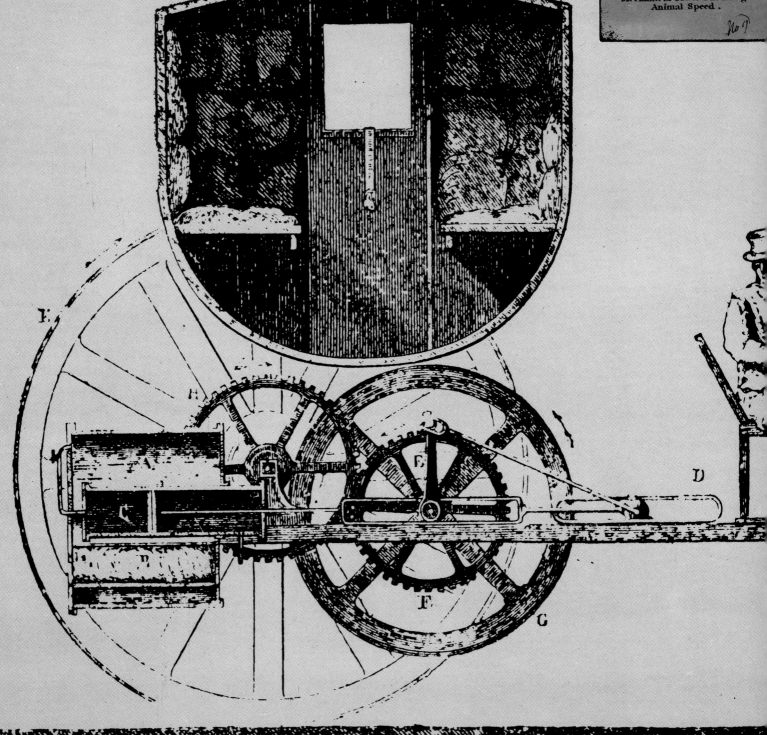

10

Left: Richard Trevithick's steam-powered *Catch-me-who-can* carriage of 1808; this, in fact, was a railway carriage. The engine was so heavy, however (it weighed about eight tons), that the timber underneath the rails sank into the ground causing the engine to overturn. Trevithick, having exhausted his finances by this stage, could not afford to have the project repaired

Below: Trevithick's Common Road Passenger Locomotive of 1803. Richard Trevithick was one of the few early steam pioneers whose products could be described as being truly practical

Bottom: Trevithick was one of the most successful of the early steam pioneers. Although he was a prolific inventor, his problem was that he seldom followed a project through to its end and when he died in 1833 he was virtually penniless

being produced'. So, Evans received an exclusive licence for the manufacture and operation of steam carriages within the State of Maryland for the fourteen years commencing May 1787.

He could not obtain financial backing for his steam carriage project – maybe his prophesies that one day people would travel in stage carriages moved by steam from one city to another almost as fast as birds could fly scared off prospective investors – so in 1801 decided to 'discharge his debt of honour to the State of Maryland by producing the steam waggons'. He had got no further than the preliminary stages of construction when he concluded that it would be more profitable to use his steam engine to drive mills. In 1805, however, he fitted wheels to a twenty-ton dredger he had built for the Board of Health of Philadelphia to convert it, albeit temporarily, to an amphibian; and the short, clumsy waddle of this '*Orukter Amphibolos*' is generally accepted as the first successful journey by a steam carriage on American soil.

However, in Europe the first truly practicable steam carriage had already made its appearance, built by the Cornish mining engineer Richard Trevithick, who had devised a high-pressure steam engine of unprecedented efficiency, and had been building experimental models of steam vehicles since 1796.

Trevithick employed several workmen in Camborne for the repair and improvement of mining engines and pumping machinery, and in November 1800 they began work in their spare time on building a full-sized road locomotive to their master's design. Some of the larger components were finished in the workshops of Trevithick's cousin and collaborator, Andrew Vivian, while other parts had been made in the cradle of the British industrial revolution at Coalbrookdale.

The single vertical cylinder was recessed into the boiler, and its piston rod was attached to a crosshead which rotated the front wheels of the carriage by means of long connecting rods. The stoker stood on a platform at the rear; this apparently turned with the back axle, which had smaller wheels than the front, to give a reasonable steering lock before they fouled the tubby boiler. By Christmas Eve, 1801, the carriage was ready for its first trials, watched by a crowd of people, one of whom subsequently set down his reminiscences of the

event: 'I knew Captain Dick Trevithick very well. I was a cooper by trade, and when Trevithick was making his steam carriage I used to go every day into John Tyack's shop in the Weith, close by here, where they put her together. In the year 1801, upon Christmas Eve, towards night, Trevithick got up steam, out on the high road, just outside the shop. When we saw that Trevithick was going to turn on steam, we jumped up as many as could, maybe seven or eight of us. 'Twas a stiffish hill going up to Camborne Beacon, but she went off like a little bird. When she had gone about a quarter of a mile, there was a rough piece of road, covered with loose stones. She did not go quite so fast, and as it was a flood of rain, and we were very much squeezed together, I jumped off. She was going faster than I could walk, and went up the hill about half a mile further, when they turned her, and came back again to the shop'.

So, and apparently with very few teething troubles, the first successful self-propelled road vehicle in history took to the roads. Over the next few days, Trevithick and Vivian made a number of short journeys in the locality of Camborne, then the carriage broke down; conveniently, as it happened, outside an inn. The two young men pushed it under a lean-to and retired to the inn,

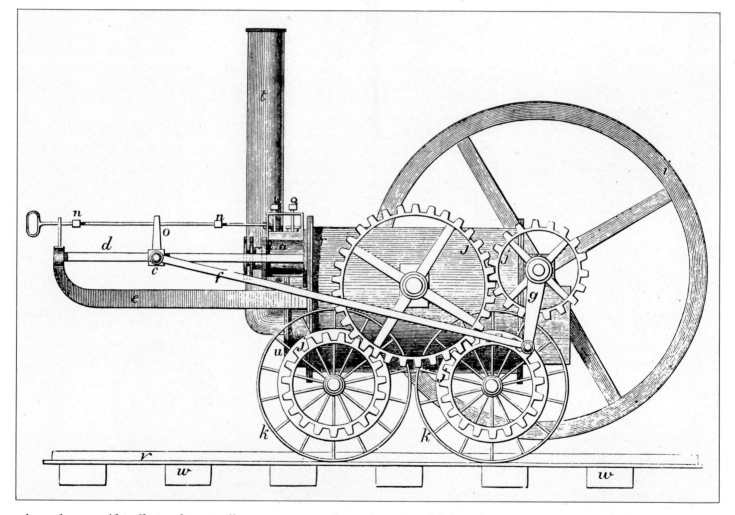

where the soporific efforts of an excellent roast goose plus appropriate drinks caused them to forget that they had failed to put out the fire in the carriage's boiler. Inevitably, the water evaporated, the iron of the boiler became red hot, and finally the wooden chassis smouldered and burned to ashes. So, too, did the lean-to . . .

Undaunted, Trevithick and Vivian journeyed to London where, on 22 March 1802, they secured a patent for high-pressure steam engines for propelling steam wagons on common roads; in 1803, they built a carriage on the lines described in the London patent in Felton's carriage shop in Leather Lane. With the boiler and cylinder at the rear, and a coach body mounted between the large-diameter rear wheels, the London carriage was a far more sophisticated design than its predecessor, and its reported achievements were correspond-

Above: another of Trevithick's ventures was this tramroad locomotive of 1803. With a load of twenty-five tons behind, it could travel at a speed of 4 mph up various inclines. Running light, though, it could attain no less than 16 mph

Right: Trevithick's first carriage was this strange railway-looking device which was constructed in 1801. After successful trials, the vehicle was left outside an inn where its happy builders went to indulge in a little light refreshment.
Unfortunately, they forgot to extinguish its fire and it burned up its chassis and the shed in which it was standing

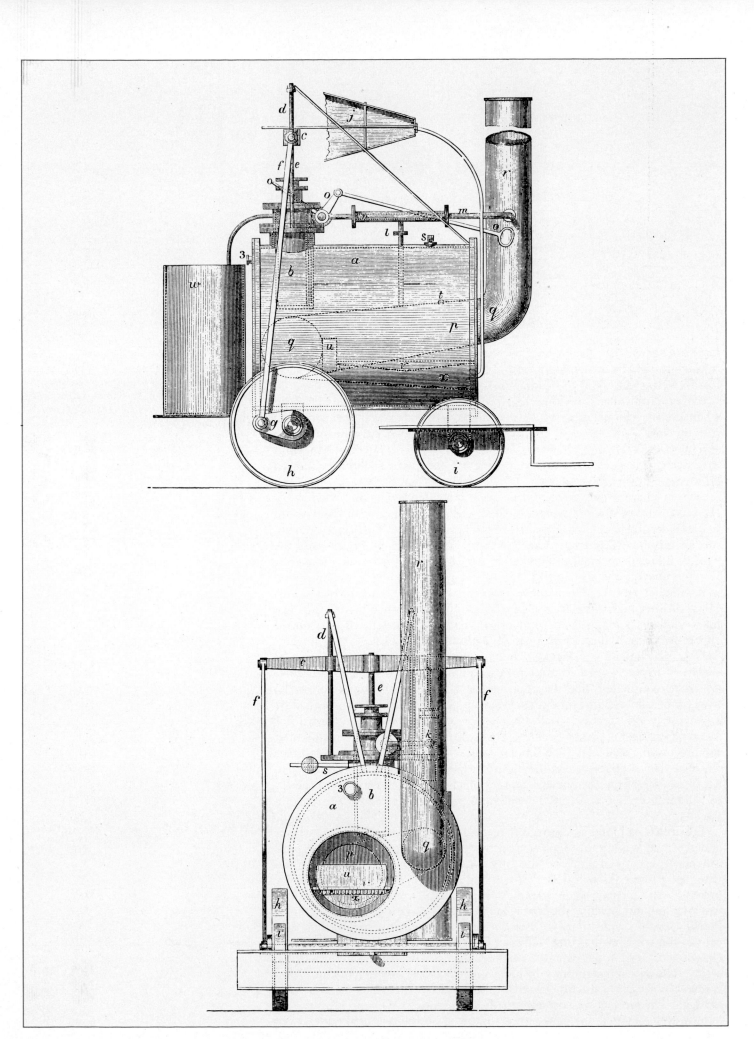

ingly greater. Vivian, for instance, is said to have made a journey of ten miles through the streets of London . . . from Leather Lane, Gray's Inn Lane, on to Lord's Cricket Ground, to Paddington, and home again by way of Islington.

Early one morning, Trevithick and Vivian were running along the City Road when Vivian, who was steering, became distracted, and allowed the carriage to run too close to the edge of the road, with the consequence that it tore down several yards of fencing. 'On one occasion, this steam coach ran through Oxford Street at a good speed, amid much cheering; no horses or vehicles were allowed on the road during the trial.'

It seems that the new carriage was a great success. The eminent scientist Sir Humphrey Davy saw it running: 'I shall soon hope to hear that the roads of England are the haunts of Captain Trevithick's dragons'. Trevithick, though, was already following a new star, and the following year he would build the world's first railway engine (he failed to persist with this invention, too). The London carriage was dismantled, and its engine sold to power a hoop rolling mill, which it continued to do for several years. Trevithick's inability to see his inventions through to perfection proved his downfall: when he died in 1833, his workmates at Hall's factory in Dartford had to club together to pay for the cost of his funeral, for he had spent all (and more) than he had.

However, he had opened the way to other inventors, although it must be admitted that for several years after the London Patent it was the lunatic fringe which predominated, like the appropriately named John Dumbell, who in 1808 proposed an engine for drawing carriages along the highway propelled by an engine in which steam would be raised by dropping water on to a red-hot metal plate, causing 'vanes, or fliers, like the sails of a windmill' to revolve and rotate a driving shaft. Or John Tindall, whose 1814 patent described a three-wheeled vehicle pushed along the highway by four steam-driven legs attached to the 'hinder part of the carriage' and supplemented by the action of 'a species of windmill, driven partly by the wind and partly by the exhaust steam from the engine'.

Trevithick had long ago proved that the adhesion between carriage wheels and the road was quite sufficient to provide traction, yet the obsession with articulated legs to circumvent wheelslip continued. In 1813, one W. Brunton patented a 'mechanical traveller' which had two legs at the rear of the boiler linked to the piston rod in such a way that they performed a continuous 'walking' motion, pushing the carriage forward in a series of jerks. In the 1820s, David Gordon made trials with elaborate leg-propelled carriages, but they proved too complex and destructive of the road surface, and the project was abandoned. Gordon also patented another splendidly lunatic machine, in which a tiny railway engine running inside a nine-foot-diameter steel drum like a squirrel in a cage formed the tractive unit for a two-wheeled steerable fore-carriage. This project was also eventually abandoned.

However, practical inventors were appearing on the scene, like the Czech

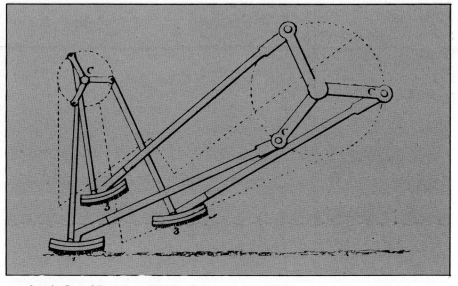

mechanic Josef Bozek, who in 1815 drove a little steam carriage, which would not have looked out of date eighty years later, through the streets of Prague. He also applied this engine to a small boat, but was ruined when the gate money taken during a demonstration of his inventions was stolen during a thunderstorm. Although his debts were later paid off by the local freemasons, Bozek destroyed his carriage and boats in disgust.

More successful was the English inventor Medhurst who, after dabbling with a 'new improved Aeolian engine' powered by compressed air, and even an artillery wagon propelled by a gunpowder engine, built a little steam carriage which, between April and July 1819, made several successful journeys along the New Road between Paddington and Islington at a speed of five miles an hour. A larger version of this machine could carry four people at a speed of seven miles an hour, but family pressures caused Medhurst to abandon his experiments in the mid 1820s.

However, he was the first of a series of inventors who, with varying degrees of success, would make the period between 1820 and 1840 the first golden age of the self-propelled vehicle.

Below: this cartoon depicting a steam-engined tricycle of 1818 can now be found in France's Conservatoire des Arts et Métiers in Paris. It seems that even in those days motorists had fuel-price problems because, in the cartoon caption, the driver is haggling over the price of a sack of coal. By 1818, of course, the Golden Age of Steam was well under way, but the vehicles produced were still 'carriages' rather than 'motor cars' as we have come to know them

CHAPTER 2

The Golden Age of Steam

The Birmingham workshops of the engineer Joseph Bramah were one of the focal points of the Industrial Revolution, a gathering place for inventors of all kinds, who would come here to compare notes and glean new ideas. Here Bramah invented the hydraulic press and the beer pump, and here Julius Griffiths had his steam carriage built in 1821. Long and massive in construction, the Griffiths carriage boasted such advanced features as a condenser to conserve its water supply and a variable-ratio final drive. Unfortunately, it also had a 'very defective boiler', and during three or four years, progressed no further than abortive tests in Bramah's yard. However, the ingenious nature of its construction served as inspiration to the other would-be steam carriage builders who visited Bramah's workshops. 'The engines, pumps and connections were all in the best style of mechanical execution, and had Mr Griffith's boiler been of such a kind as to generate regularly the required quantity of steam, a perfect steam carriage must have been the result.'

In 1824, Timothy Burstall (ominous name!) and John Hill began work on a steam carriage, which underwent trials at Leith and Edinburgh in 1826, and in London in 1827. Again, this was a machine whose technical specification promised far more than the mediocre results of its test runs, for it was the first vehicle in history to feature four-wheel drive. A complicated system of bevel gearing permitted the front wheels to be steered as well as powered, and this was also the first shaft-driven road vehicle in history. Moreover, it had front-wheel brakes and a silencer and, according to an account in the *Edinburgh Philosophical Journal*, may well have had the first flash boiler. 'They proposed to heat (the boiler) from 250°F to 600°F and, by keeping the water in a separate vessel, and only applying it to the boiler when steam was wanted, they accomplished that desideratum of making just such a quantity of steam as was wanted; so that when going down hill all the steam and heat might be saved, to be accumulated and given out again at the first hill or piece of rough road when, more being wanted, more will be expended.'

Against all these advanced features were set the facts that Burstall & Hill's machine was powered by an archaic side-beam engine of the type normally used in paddle-steamers, and that it weighed an earth-shaking eight tons. Consequently, the carriage was incapable of moving at speeds greater than three or four miles an hour, and even that put so much strain on the boiler that it burst.

Undaunted, Burstall & Hill then announced a new project, for a two-wheeled 'power pack' to carry the boiler separate from the main body of the carriage, to allay the fears of passengers that there might be an explosion; a quarter-scale model of this machine, with six wheels, of which the centre pair drove, was demonstrated in Edinburgh and London. It seems that trials with a full-size version were unsuccessful, and that the boiler and engine were then removed and fitted in a railway locomotive, the *Perseverance*, which was entered for – and almost immediately withdrawn from – the Rainhill locomotive trials of 1829, where Stevenson's *Rocket* emerged victorious.

In 1824, William Henry James, of Thavies Inn, Holborn, London, a 'gentleman of superior mechanical talents', was the first steam carriage designer to attempt to give some positive form of differential action to the driving wheels, having realised that on a corner the outer wheel travelled further than the inner. Others, like Burstall and Hill, had arranged a sort of 'differential by default' in which ratchets in the hubs permitted the drive to the outer wheel to be over-ridden on curves (small wonder that their four-wheel-drive carriage was so troublesome!), but James proposed a far more commendable solution which, in model form at least, worked quite successfully. Each rear wheel had its own cranked half axle driven by a twin-cylinder engine working at high pressure; on the front axle were cocks which were opened and closed as the carriage turned, automatically controlling the amount of steam passing to each engine, so that when the carriage was running straight, both engines received the same quantity, but on corners the outer engine received more and therefore travelled faster thus adding to its efficiency.

Writing in the *Register of Arts* in 1829, Luke Herbert recalled that the model was 'so efficient that the carriage could be made to describe every variety of

Below: a painting of Gurney's steam carriage as it appeared at Hounslow on 12 August 1829; it towed a barouche containing, among other distinguished people, the Duke of Wellington. Goldsworthy Gurney was a prolific inventor who had the ability to promote his own products and was eventually knighted for his services in improving the heating and lighting of the House of Commons. Gurney's first steam carriage used both wheels and legs for movement. In 1825, he began work on a second carriage and this was used for a nine-mile trip from London to Edgware. By 1826, Gurney had produced a monstrous steam coach which attracted a lot of public interest and comment

Left: James' steam-carriage of 1824, built by William Henry James of Thavies Inn, Holborn, who was the first steam-carriage designer to give some form of differential action to the wheels, having realised that the outer wheel travelled further than the inner when cornering. Unfortunately, James had no capital to construct a larger and more advanced design. In 1829, however, he received a commission from Sir James Anderson to construct a new vehicle based on the 1824 design

curve; he has seen it repeatedly make turns of less than ten feet radius'.

James had not then the capital to construct his design on a larger scale, but eventually received a commission from Sir James Anderson, Bart, of Buttevant Castle, Ireland, and in March 1829 they carried out experiments with a steam diligence built on the lines of James's 1824 model. On every test, some fault in design or construction had to be altered, but eventually the machine was judged ready for road travel, and 'loaded with fifteen passengers and propelled several miles on a rough gravel road across Epping Forest, with a speed varying from twelve to fifteen miles an hour'. Then a boiler tube split, letting the water out of one of the boilers and extinguishing its fire.

'Under these circumstances', wrote Luke Hebert in *Galloway's Treatise on the Steam Engine*, 'with only one boiler in operation, the carriage returned home at the rate of about seven miles an hour, carrying more than twenty passengers, at one period, indeed, it is said, a much greater number; showing that sufficient steam can be generated in such a boiler to be equal to the propulsion of between five tons and six tons weight. In consequence of this flattering demonstration that the most brilliant success was obtainable, the proprietors dismantled the carriage and commenced the construction of superior tubular boilers with much stronger tubes.'

In fact, what emerged after the rebuild was an entirely new, and much less complicated, machine, intended to replace the team of horses in front of a stagecoach, and to which end the novelty of a two-speed transmission was provided.

In one of the very first road-test articles, which appeared in the *Mechanics' Magazine* in November 1829, the author commented: 'A series of interesting experiments were made throughout the whole of yesterday with a new carriage belonging to Sir James Anderson, Bart, and W. H. James, Esq, on the Vauxhall, Kensington and Clapham roads, with the view of ascertaining the practical advantages of some perfectly novel apparatus attached to the engines, the results of which were so satisfactory that the proprietors intend immediately establishing several stage coaches on the principle. The writer was favoured with a ride during the last experiment, when the machine proceeded from Vauxhall Bridge to the Swan at Clapham, a distance of two and a half miles, which was run at the rate of fifteen miles an hour. From what I had the pleasure of witnessing, I am confident that this carriage is far superior to every other locomotive carriage hitherto brought before the public, and that she will easily perform fifteen miles an hour throughout a long journey. The body of the carriage, if not elegant, is neat, being the figure of a parallelogram. It is a very small and compact machine, and runs upon four wheels'.

It seems that once again the workmanship of the day was not up to coping with the very high steam pressures used by James, though, for the new carriage rarely managed to run for more than three or four miles without one or other of its steam joints breaking.

James's last carriage was patented in 1832, and had a three-speed chain transmission, with the ratios changed by pedals. It seems that around the same time Anderson ran out of money, and this design was never built.

A carriage which attracted far less attention than that of James, yet which enjoyed far greater success, was constructed around the year 1827 by the young engineer James Nasmyth, who was then little more than a boy, being only some nineteen years old.

'Having made a small working model of a steam carriage,' he recalled, 'I exhibited it before the members of the Scottish Society of Arts. The performance of this active little machine was so gratifying to the Society that they requested me to construct one of such power as to enable four or six persons to be conveyed along the ordinary roads. The members of the Society, in their individual capacity, subscribed £60, which they placed in my hands as the means for carrying out their project. I accordingly set to work at once, and completed the carriage in about four months, when it was exhibited before the members of the Society of Arts. Many successful trials were made with it on the Queensferry Road near Edinburgh. The runs were generally of four or five miles, with a load of eight passengers sitting on benches about three feet from

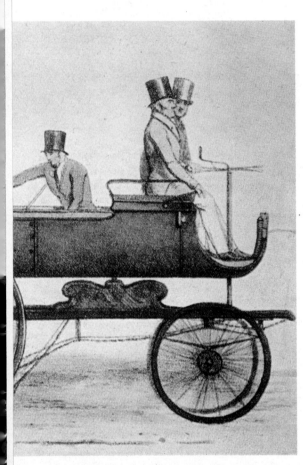

bore and 12 in stroke, was reputedly capable of reaching 32 mph and, according to a correspondent in the *Saturday Magazine*, was reliable enough to cover quite considerable distances without mishap. 'I have just returned from witnessing the triumph of science in mechanics, by travelling along a hilly and crooked road from Oxford to Birmingham in a steam carriage. This truly wonderful machine is the invention of Captain Ogle, of the Royal Navy, and Mr Summers, his partner, and is the first and only one that has accomplished so long a journey over chance roads and without rails. Its rate of travelling may be called twelve miles an hour, but twenty or perhaps thirty down hill if not checked by the brake, a contrivance which places the whole of the machinery under complete control. Away went the splendid vehicle through that beauteous city (Oxford) at the rate of ten miles an hour which, when clear of the houses, was accelerated to fourteen. Just as the steam carriage was entering the town of Birmingham, the supply of coke being exhausted, the steam dropped; and the good people, on learning the cause, flew to the frame, and dragged it into the yard.'

Like other pioneers, though, Ogle and Summers seem not to have persisted once they had achieved a long-distance journey. They were at least more successful than the notorious Doctor Church of Birmingham who, with backing from a group of optimists calling themselves the London and Birmingham Steam Carriage Company, sanguinely hoped to inaugurate a regular road service linking the two cities. If contemporary engravings are to be believed, Church's steam carriage was a massive rococo three-wheeler running on wheels with wide 'elastic rims' that 'bent into "flatted curves" as they came in contact with the ground, thereby preventing the wheels from sinking or sliding round'; it could carry fifty passengers.

The behemoth which was designed by one Doctor Church of Birmingham in 1833. This engraving depicts the fifty-seat vehicle travelling under its own steam in service, whereas in reality it only ran on two tests, and one of those ended ignominiously, with the carriage being towed by the horses it was supposed to replace

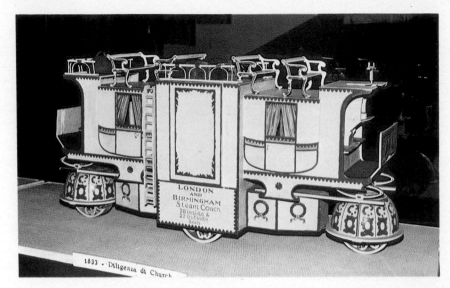

1833 - Diligenza di Church

Far left: a scale model of Doctor Church's steam coach depicted in the previous engraving; this miniature version can be found in the Turin Automobile Museum

Left and below: the steam carriage of Messrs Macerone and Squire, constructed in 1833. The builders were proud of their machine, and their works were always open to 'editors of newspapers, engineers and other scientific persons'. On one trip to Bushey Heath and Watford, the vehicle thundered downhill at the incredible speed of 30 mph. It was noted that Mr Squire, steering, 'never lost his presence of mind'

Even if the carriage was completed in this manner, its total public appearances were limited to two short test runs, one of which ended with the vehicle being hauled back to the works behind horses. However, within a few months, the London and Birmingham Steam Carriage Company optimistically advertised that 'all the difficulties of running steam carriages upon common roads were now overcome, and would be done to great profit to those engaged in it'.

'It was wisely suggested', noted one commentator, 'that instead of puffing and advertising, the company should put a carriage on the road at once for passenger traffic between Birmingham and London; but this scheme was never practically accomplished; the carriages were constantly brought out, and as constantly failed.'

Failure of a different and more tragic kind was the lot of Francis Macerone, an Anglo-Italian born in Manchester in 1788, whose early life was a series of wild adventures, culminating in his being appointed aide-de-camp to the King of Naples in 1814. Somewhere along the way he acquired the rank of Colonel and a taste for speed, fostered by the many breakneck horse rides he had undertaken.

In 1825, he became assistant to Goldsworthy Gurney in London, but after four years he had become convinced that Gurney's efforts would never succeed, and left the steam carriage business to go to Constantinople to fight for the Turks against the Russians. He remained there until 1831, then returned to England. Then, recalled Macerone: 'Mr J. Squire came to me and informed me that he had built a steam carriage, which performed very well, and asked me to join him in the undertaking. Finding the little carriage much superior to any that Gurney had made, but unfortunately fitted with a very defective boiler, I undertook to join in the construction of another on my plan, for which a valid patent could be obtained, but I was without much money, having, through the "fortunes of war", returned from Turkey with even less than I went with. However, I mentioned my dilemma to a gentleman, the like of whom there are too few in this world, who provided me with the funds for taking convenient premises, purchasing lathes, tools, and establishing a factory on the Paddington Wharf. I placed Mr Squire in the house on the works as foreman, and we set to work on an enlarged scale'.

Macerone and Squire completed their first steam carriage in 1833 in a blaze of publicity; the works at Paddington were always open house to 'editors of newspapers, engineers and other scientific persons', who were encouraged to take rides on the vehicle, and its numerous trials were widely reported. It seems to have been a remarkable performer, with its turn of speed testified to by many accounts in the press.

One of the best descriptions of the machine appeared in *Turner's Annual Tour* for 1834. 'Drawn out of a hut on Bushey Heath by the appearance of an unusual commotion amongst the inhabitants of the village, we saw a steam coach which stopped there. The apparition of a vehicle of this kind, in such a place, was unaccountable. Bushey Heath forms the plateau of a mountain, which is the highest point of land in Middlesex and, although so far inland, serves as a landmark for vessels at sea. The access to it, from the London side, is by a difficult and steep road. Being accosted by Colonel Macerone, in whom we were glad to recognise an old acquaintance, he informed us that the journey had been performed with ease, adding that it was his intention to proceed to the town of Watford.

'Now, if the road from Edgware to Bushey Heath was steep and difficult, the descent from Bushey Heath to Watford was much worse. We told our friend that he might go by steam to Watford, but that we were quite certain that he would not return by the same means of locomotion. Nevertheless, at his pressing instance, we consented to hazard our own person in the adventure. We set off, amidst the cheers of the villagers. The motion was so steady that we could have read with ease, and the noise was no worse than that produced by a common vehicle. On arriving at the summit of Clay Hill, the local and in-experienced attendant neglected to clog the wheel until it become impossible. We went thundering down the hill at the rate of thirty miles an hour. Mr Squire was steersman, and never lost his presence of mind. It may be conceived what amazement a thing of this kind, flashing through the village of Bushey, occas-ioned among the inhabitants. The people seemed petrified on seeing a carriage without horses. In the busy and populous town of Watford the sensation was similar – the men gazed in speechless wonder; the women clapped their hands. We turned round at the end of the street in magnificent style, and ascended Clay Hill at the same rate as the stage coaches drawn by five horses, and at length regained our starting place.'

This was the high point in Macerone's career. In 1834, he quarrelled with Squire, who left the business. Finding himself short of cash, Macerone entered into a dangerously vague agreement with one D'Asda, an 'Italian Jew and audacious adventurer', who was anxious to exhibit the two steam carriages built by Macerone on the Continent. D'Asda promised that Macerone would be paid £1500 for a share of the patents he would take out in France and Belgium and, accordingly, the carriages were sent to Brussels and Paris for exhibition runs.

In Paris, D'Asda displayed the carriage in front of the King and Queen, who were much impressed with this 'French invention' which the audacious adventurer had shamelessly claimed had been built to his order by a French engineer named Clavière; their Majesties were so impressed that they gave D'Asda a gold snuff-box bearing the Royal Arms, and he subsequently sold his 'rights' in the steam carriage for £16,000, of which poor Macerone saw not a solitary penny.

Macerone's creditors stripped the Paddington factory bare, leaving the unfortunate engineer scarcely enough to exist on. Because he had no demon-stration vehicles, his attempts to form a new steam carriage company were doomed to failure. It was only in 1841 that a new Macerone carriage was built, for the General Steam Carriage Company. Macerone had contracted to supply the company with carriages for £800 each, but the engineer who built the prototype put in a bill of £1100 to cover the cost of alterations and experimental trips. Although the machine ran reliably and climbed Shooter's Hill, Black-heath, at a speed which 'delighted several shareholders', the Steam Carriage company refused to pay the engineer's bills; he, in turn, locked the machine away and refused to let it go on the roads again. Caught in the middle of this argument was the unfortunate Macerone, all of whose possessions were seized by his creditors.

He tried to sell his boiler patents to raise capital, but to no avail. The name of Macerone failed to figure in the subsequent history of steam traction, although his former collaborator, Squire, proposed an eleven-seater charabanc in 1843. The design of its boiler prompted an angry letter from Macerone in the *Mechanic's Magazine*, claiming that Squire had infringed his (obviously unsold) patent.

Around this time, a German engineer named Jean-Christian Dietz, who had come to France during the reign of Napoleon to build canals, was developing, along with his sons Charles and Christian, a series of improbable-looking

'The Progress of Steam: Alken's illustration of modern prophecy.' This illustration, with its cynical overtones, depicts Whitechapel Road, East London, in 1830. The prophecy of mobile canteens and vendors' vehicles is accurate, as is the pollution and smoke that is seen hanging low over the area. It was, however, left to the petrol-engine-powered vehicle to fit the bill. Road racing, represented by the *Infernal Defiance of Yarmouth* passing the *Dreadful Vengence of Colchester*, was also to be seen in later years *remorquers*, which were little more than road-going railway engines of great bulk and complexity, intended to draw great strings of carriages along the public highways.

In 1834, Charles Dietz gave a display of one of these *remorquers* in Paris, where it drew two three-wheeled carriages along the Champs-Elysees and out into the suburbs. Riding among the forty distinguished guests in the carriages was one Odolant Desnos, who effused: 'This glorious arrival of M. Dietz, since such results have hitherto not been achieved in France, was to the travellers a spectacle as brilliant as it was novel. No words can describe the magnificent picture afforded by the immense crowd which so covered the route that . . . the carriage could scarcely clear a passage. It was a triumphal progress . . .'.

On the spot, the Academie de l'Industrie awarded Dietz their gold medal. Other outings, though, were not so successful. In 1841 Christian Dietz attempted to run a regular service between Bordeaux and Libourn, but he was met with such open hostility from the local carriers that on one occasion he was forced to beat off attackers with his poker. Soon afterwards, the Dietz family ceased their experiments with steam traction.

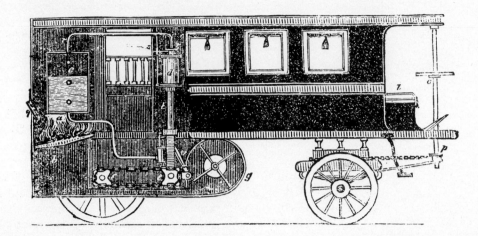

Left: the workings of Hancock's *Infant* of 1830, in its early, closed, form; after the machine blew up, it was rebuilt with a longer wheelbase, in an effort to improve it

Below: Walter Hancock produced these vehicles in his Stratford, East London, workshop; they are the rebuilt *Infant*, the *Era* and the *Autopsy*. *Infant* was 'the first steam coach that ever carried passengers for hire, or made the journey to Brighton, or passed through the City of London by steam'. *Autopsy* also made the Brighton trip and, like *Infant*, travelled 'thousands of miles'. *Era* was built for the London-to-Greenwich route, as opposed to that from London to Paddington travelled by the two other vehicles

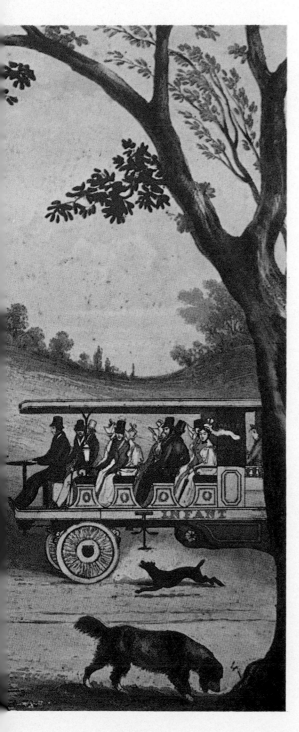

However, the man who dominated this first steam age, and whose career successfully spanned it from start to finish, was Walter Hancock of Stratford, which was then a village on the eastern outskirts of London. Hancock had been born in Marlborough, Wiltshire, in 1799, and first turned his attention to the construction of steam carriages in 1824. His brother, Thomas, had pioneered the manufacture of vulcanised rubber goods, and this prompted Walter Hancock to devise an ingenious, if unsuccessful, power unit in which pistons and cylinders were replaced by rubber bags linked to a crankshaft; they were alternately blow up with steam and then deflated to rotate the crank. A carriage with this type of power unit was built, but refused to run.

Hancock's experiments really began to bear fruit in 1827, when he devised a new and more efficient design of boiler, which was installed in a little three-wheeled carriage which had a pair of oscillating cylinders of conventional design driving the single front wheel (which also steered). This carriage was really a mobile test bed for Hancock's ideas, and its design was altered many times; despite this, it covered several hundred miles, 'sometimes to Epping Forest, at other times to Paddington, and frequently to Whitechapel. On one occasion it ran to Hounslow, and on another to Croydon. In every instance, it accomplished the task assigned to it, and returned to Stratford on the same day on which it set out. Subsequently, this carriage went from Stratford, through Pentonville, to Turnham Green, over Hammersmith Bridge, and thence to Fulham. In that neighbourhood, it remained several days, and made a number of excursions in different directions, for the gratification of some of Hancock's friends, and others who had expressed a desire to witness its performance'.

Hancock's next design, which appeared in 1830, was a far more sophisticated machine. Named the *Infant*, it was a covered char-à-bancs with seats for ten passengers. Although it retained the oscillating engine, this was now placed at the rear of the machine, and drove the back axle through a chain.

In 1831, Hancock began running a regular service between Stratford and London with the *Infant*, which had already shown its merits in an assault on the 1-in-20 slope of Pentonville Hill. Hancock later wrote: 'A severe frost following a shower of sleet had completely glazed the road, so that horses could scarcely keep their footing. The trial was made therefore under the most unfavourable circumstances possible; so much so, that confident as the writer felt in the powers of his engine, his heart inclined to fail him. The carriage, however, did its duty nobly. Without the aid of propellers or any other such appendages (then thought necessary on a level road), the hill was ascended at considerable speed and the summit successfully attained, while his competitors with their horses were yet but a little way from the bottom of the hill'.

It was while *Infant* was operating its fare-paying service that its stoker (the French were already calling such men *chauffeurs*) decided that it would be an excellent idea to wire the safety valve shut and run the engine declutched from the transmission to get the fire really glowing with its blower fan, and thus build up a good head of steam for the restart. Unfortunately, it also created sufficient pressure to rupture the boiler, and the unfortunate stoker dropped dead with surprise! Hancock claimed, somewhat unbelievably, that none of the passengers noticed the incident . . .

In 1832, Hancock decided to remedy the many imperfections in the design of *Infant* by a rebuild, with the result that an almost totally new carriage was created, longer in the wheelbase and equipped with an extra row of seats. Most importantly, the power unit, which had previously operated in the full blast of the road dirt thrown up by the rear wheels, was replaced by a fixed twin-cylinder engine housed within the bodywork of the vehicle. The reborn *Infant* was used for the first-ever motorised seaside outing, on which Hancock took eleven 'scientific gentlemen' – including Alexander Gordon, who had just launched the world's first motoring magazine, *The Journal of Elemental Locomotion*, and would in 1833 form a short-lived 'motor club'.

A 'London & Brighton Steam Carriage Company' was formed, and Hancock constructed a closed carriage called *Era* for their projected London–Greenwich service (which, like so many steam-carriage promotions, failed to reach reality). In 1833, two more carriages, *Enterprise* and *Autopsy* were built – *Autopsy's* curious name meant, literally, 'see for yourself' in the original Greek, although passengers lacking the benefits of a classical education may have felt some apprehension . . .

In April 1833, *Enterprise*, which bore a closed omnibus body, began a short regular service between Moorgate and Paddington, over a route which had seen, only four years previously, the début of the first horse-drawn omnibus.

Announced Hancock: 'It is not intended to run this carriage more than about a week longer; partly because it was only intended as a demonstration of its efficiency, and partly because my own occupation will not admit of my personal attention to the steering, which I have hitherto performed myself, having no other person at present to whose guidance I could, with propriety, entrust it'.

So the service lasted only a fortnight, with *Enterprise* covering its ten-mile round trip within an hour. In that time, the regular and reliable working of the carriage aroused bitter opposition among users of horsed vehicles, who saw, somewhat prematurely, a threat to their livelihood. Complained a correspondent to the daily press: 'In watching, as I have done, the early operations of the new steam coach, the *Enterprise*, on the Paddington Road, I have been pained,

Hancock's *Enterprise* stayed in service for a mere two weeks, between Moorgate and Paddington, because Mr Hancock did not have time to do all the driving himself, and would not let any other person control the machine. Horse-drawn vehicles tended either to get in the *Enterprise*'s way or to chase it; one is seen here in full pursuit of the Omnibus-bodied carriage

the heavy piston fell and turned the wheels. The ignition, interestingly enough, was by electricity, provided by a Voltaic battery.

It seems that De Rivaz actually constructed a crude chariot on the lines described in his patent, and persuaded it to run the width of a room.

'The bother of putting the chariot back in position at the end of each trial persuaded me to have a fire engine built . . .'

In 1820 an English clergyman, the Reverend William Cecil, demonstrated a little model gas engine to the Cambridge Philosophical Society; running on hydrogen, it operated rather like a primitive steam engine, and turned at a leisurely 16 rpm. Its inventor suggested that illuminating gas, vaporised petroleum, turpentine or alcohol were possible alternative fuels. Although he did not apply his engine to any more exciting use than pumping water, Cecil directed the attention of those who were beginning to experiment with road carriages towards the use of gas engines.

David Gordon, indeed, proposed that vehicles could be propelled by compressed coal gas delivered to refuelling stations round the country in pressurised containers, but abandoned this scheme when he computed the

Barsanti, Matteuchi and a model of their first gas engine, patented on 13 May 1854; the twin pistons were set free in the cylinders and drove, via rack rods, a flywheel shaft; the unit's first public demonstration was in 1856 and Barsanti commented: 'This machine was enough to announce that before long the power of steam would be replaced by a perfect, inexpensive motive force'

Above: the first steam wagon to go into public service in France was this tug, designed by Charles Dietz and seen here towing a coach full of passengers in the Champs Elysées in 1834

operating costs to be prohibitively expensive.

Perhaps the most successful disciple of the Reverend Cecil was Samuel Brown, of Brompton, who in 1824 began experiments with a 'gas-and-vacuum' engine. In 1826 he mounted a developed version of this power unit, which had twin cylinders linked by a rocking beam, in a four-wheeled chariot. This was tested on the open road in May of that year, and climbed the slope of Shooters Hill, near Woolwich, 'to the astonishment of numerous spectators'. Once again, excessive operating costs were the rock on which this venture foundered, and Brown then turned his attention to employing his engine to drive canal boats; although he constructed a paddle steamer which ran on the Thames, Brown found that on water, too, gas power was too expensive.

Another form of motive power which was engaging the attention of inventors at this period was compressed air, and here the most ingenious suggestions were made by William Mann, of Brixton, who, after three years of experiment, published a pamphlet in 1830 in which he proposed a system of 'power stations' at intervals of 15 to 20 miles along the main carriage routes. Alternatively, he suggested a continuous iron main with power stations in the coal districts.

Mann intended that the carriages operating under his system should carry a supply of air in cylinders, each of around 5 cu ft capacity. Equipped with fifteen such cylinders, pressurised to 32 atmospheres, the carriage would, he claimed, run for 14 miles; at a pressure of 64 atmospheres, 34 miles could be covered at an average cost of a penny a mile.

'It would be well,' thought Mann, 'to make persons confined in Clerkenwell and other prisons earn their dinners by compressing air for the supplying of power for propelling His Majesty's Mails throughout the kingdom.' However, neither Mann, nor his contemporary, Wright, who patented a carriage powered by a combination of compressed air and steam, seems to have realised such designs in a practicable form.

It was not until the 1850s that a viable alternative to steam power for road vehicles became available. It had long been known that certain gases – notably oxygen and hydrogen – could be combined in certain proportions and ignited within a closed container to give a powerful explosion. The difficulty lay in harnessing the power of that explosion, as De Rivaz had found.

The first practicable gas engine was patented in 1853 by two Italians, Barsanti and Matteucci, who, ignorant of the attempts that had been made in earlier years to construct power units of this type, believed themselves to be the orignal inventors of the gas engine. The concept was actually that of Eugenio Barsanti, a priest who taught at a secondary school in Florence; he was the theorist and Felice Matteucci was the engineer who translated his ideas into metal.

Barsanti had conceived a twin-cylinder engine with free pistons carrying rack-rods which rotated a flywheel shaft as they operated on a complex three-

45

CHAPTER 4

The Birth of an Industry

Left: the Scotte steam carriage of 1892, which had a top speed of 12 kph; for what is really a very late design in the steam-vehicle field, this performance seems pathetic; this was, after all, at a time when there were far more sophisticated petroleum-powered vehicles on the road

To its fond parents, the motor car was now a commercial proposition, but, for a prospective purchaser, to buy one would be an awfully big adventure. When, in 1888, Emile Roger took his new Benz away from the works, he had been personally coached in its care and maintenance by 'Papa Benz' himself. After it had been duly transported back to Paris, however, the car refused to start, and Benz had to follow it, to instruct a mechanic in its handling. Curiously enough, Roger had garaged his car in the workshop of Panhard & Levassor, who also manufactured Benz two-stroke engines under licence, in addition to their Daimler activities. They showed as little interest in the vehicle as did the rest of the public, and no sale was forthcoming.

To Benz's partners, Rose and Esslinger, his preoccupation with the motor vehicle was becoming a threat to the business. 'Herr Benz', Rose would complain, 'we've now made a nice pile of money, but you had best keep your fingers out of that motor car or you'll lose everything'. Then he would sigh and add 'My God, my God, where is this all going to end?'.

It ended for Rose and Esslinger in 1890, when they resigned from the company, to be replaced by two more accommodating businessmen, Von Fischer and Ganss, who had useful experience of selling in foreign markets. From then on, progress, if not swift, was at least positive.

On New Year's Day 1891, a postmaster named Kugler wrote to Benz, intrigued by the latter's suggestion that the motor car might prove useful to the postal authorities. 'I am positive that your ingenious and most practical inven-

Right: a Benz of 1888. The single-cylinder, four-stroke engine produced around $1\frac{1}{2}$ hp between 250 and 300 rpm and drove the generously proportioned rear wheels through chains. This is the car about the intricacies of which 'Papa Benz' coached its owner, Emile Roger

Left: steel wire wheels gave this car, which Daimler sent to the 1889 Paris World Fair, the name 'Stahlradwagen'. A $1\frac{1}{2}$ hp, 'high-speed', vee-twin motor, of Daimler's own design, was fitted in the rear of a two-seater, tubular-steel, four-wheeled chassis. The car was instrumental in influencing Peugeot and Panhard & Levassor to begin production of Daimler-engined vehicles in France

Below: an example of the 1893 Benz Viktoria, the first four-wheeled car built by the company. The cars' single-cylinder engine produced 3 bhp at 700 rpm and could propel the vehicles at 25 kph. The world's first production car, the 1894 Benz Velo was based on the Viktoria design

tion will be crowned with a great success, I am not only thinking of its usefulness to the postal services, but I am utterly convinced that it would be most excellent for a country doctor. Not every doctor in a small village has box stalls, horses and a farm to maintain them, yet some kind of a cart is essential for a doctor who has to make calls in a number of places distant from each other. How often is a doctor called on during the night, and how else is he meant to get where he has to go? Before he has roused the sleep-drunk peasant from his bed and got him to put the bridle and harness on the horse, a lot of valuable time has been lost.

'There is another thing about your vehicle: it comes to a halt and turns off and that's it. It doesn't need any feed, or any groom, no blacksmith, no danger of having a horse shy; it just moves along as though a ghostly hand were pushing it—and one stroke of the brakes and it stops. That is what makes it so inexpensive to operate. Even the stupidest blockhead must be able to see such an immense advantage as this.

'The vehicle in motion does have something comical in its appearance from the aesthetic point of view, and someone who did not know what it was might think it was a runaway chaise he was looking at. That is because we have not yet grown used to it.

'But here also, in my opinion, a lot of minor changes and adjustments can artfully be made to improve its appearance without in any way losing sight of the characteristics that serve its purpose. If this were done, the lack of an animal in front to pull it would not be so striking to the beholder.'

Benz was, indeed, already planning changes, most important of which was the development of a four-wheeled car with geometrically accurate steering; meanwhile, the automobile workshop at Mannheim was concentrating mainly on the production of motor boats, which were proving quite popular in Germany. In 1893, the first Benz four-wheeler was ready to be put on the market; its inventor called it the 'Viktoria' because it represented victory over a tricky design problem (he was, apparently, ignorant of the invention of the king-pin steering system patented in 1816 by Georg Lankensperger—coachbuilder to the Royal Court of Bavaria—and later pirated by Rudolf Ackermann).

It was also the first time that a car had been endowed with a glamorous model name, and really marks the beginning of serious sales of motor vehicles to the public, for Benz put the Viktoria into series production.

It was a heavier-looking vehicle than the old three-wheeler, and had a 3 hp engine with a vertical flywheel, which was easier to pull over to start the engine, and which presumably did not upset the new improved steering.

Obviously alarmed by the spectre of motor car-choked roads, the Minister of the Interior of the Grand Duchy of Baden formulated regulations governing the behaviour of automobiles on highways, which he forwarded to the Benz company at the end of November 1893: '. . . Speed on the open road shall not exceed twelve kilometres per hour outside the towns, and within town limits and around sharp corners it shall not exceed six kilometres per hour . . . Upon meeting carts, dray animals or saddle horses, road speed shall be even further diminished . . . The probationary permission being granted to drive motor vehicles on public roads, extending from 1 January to 31 December 1894, inclusive, may be withdrawn immediately in the interest of public order and safety, or further restrictive conditions may be added'.

Benz managed to get the authorities to take the sting out of these regulations, but his annual production was hardly enough to cause any road congestion problems, nor were the few owners of motor cars keen enough (or foolhardy enough) to undertake long journeys.

An exception to this was the rich German industrialist Theodor von Liebig, who in July 1894 drove his Viktoria from Reichenburg, Bohemia, *via* Mannheim and Gondorf, on the Moselle, to Reims and back. The trip was not exactly trouble free, and he only kept note of his progress as far as Gondorf, where he computed that he had used 140 kg of gasoline to travel 939 kilometres, and that the radiator had consumed 1500 litres of water. Von Liebig, though, concluded that the journey had revealed 'the delight of passing through beautiful landscape by an entirely new means of transportation', and had thus been well worth while.

A fine example of Peugeot's early *vis-a-vis*
design, albeit with more ornate bodywork than
would be normal. These vehicles had engines of
1018 cc and could attain a speed of 30 kph. This
particular example was built in 1892, along with
28 other cars
(Peugeot Collection, France)

Left: an 1894 Peugeot tourer, with trimmings characteristic of that company; as with most early Peugeots, it used handlebar steering, a tabular chassis (in which the cooling water passed) and a Daimler V-twin engine mounted at the rear

Benz, as can be seen from inventions as diverse as the Wright Flyer, the Edison Phonograph and the Ford Model T, all of which were produced long after progress had rendered them obsolescent.

However, compared with the cars being turned out by Gottlieb Daimler, the Benz Velo was the height of modernity. Daimler had signed contracts with a gunpowder manufacturer named Max Duttenhofer and another industrialist, W. Lorenz, to gain the necessary capital for expansion of his engine-building activities, a move which resulted in the formation of the Daimler-Motoren-Gesellschaft on 28 November 1890. Daimler and his new partners soon fell out, though, and at the end of 1892 he and Maybach broke away from the company to set up their own experimental workshop in the great summer hall of the defunct Hotel Hermann in Cannstatt. Here they developed the successor to the V-twin power unit, an equally outstanding engine which they called the Phönix. This had two cylinders in line, and was fitted with Maybach's new invention, the spray carburettor, which adjusted the gas/air mixture according to the engine speed and the load imposed on the power unit. This seems to have been an excessive amount of refinement for the inflexible tube-ignition system, which was happiest running at a constant speed.

Having developed an excellent power unit, Daimler and Maybach then totally nullified their achievement by fitting it in a belt-driven car of unbelievably retrograde design, which remained in production even after Daimler and his partners had resolved their quarrel, in 1895. It is hard to comprehend how Maybach could have produced this clumsy vehicle, with its centre-pivot steering, in 1893, when only seven years later he was to conceive the most advanced car in the world.

In fact, it could be argued that the principal effect of all this hard work by the Germans was to establish the French as the world's leading motor manufacturers for the ensuing decade, for the French were willing to experiment and alter, while the Germans seemed content to progress along the lines that they had established several years earlier. The French, too, seemed far more confident of the potential of the motor vehicle: in 1891, Peugeot dispatched one of their earliest cars on an ambitious foray, following the competitors in the 2047 km Paris–Brest–Paris cycle race. It covered the distance in 139 hours, 'without a moment's trouble', a feat which helped Peugeot to sell five cars to private owners that year, and to boost output to 29 in 1892.

The cars which Peugeot were making echoed the company's long experience in cycle manufacture, with tubular chassis (through which the cooling water for the engine circulated) and spindly spoked wheels. The rear-mounted Daimler engines were purchased through Panhard and Levassor until Peugeot developed their own power unit in 1896.

Having seen the results obtained by his friend Peugeot, Levassor decided to build a horseless carriage for himself, prompted, it seems, by his go-ahead wife, the former Mme Sarazin.

The first Panhard & Levassor car appeared in the late summer of 1890. It was a dogcart with the engine mounted between the seats, similar in conception to the original Daimler carriage of 1886. It was not, apparently, an unqualified success, and Levassor would grumble gently: 'If Daimler can make a carriage run at eighteen kilometres an hour, so can I . . .'

After building a couple of cars with the engine at the rear, Levassor settled on a front-engined layout, with the unit contained under a square bonnet, driving through the famous '*brusque et brutale*' gearbox (which had four speeds forward, four speeds in reverse, and operated completely *al fresco*, devoid of any protective—or oil-retaining—casing) to the countershaft and side chains which gave the final drive.

'Build heavy', said Levassor, 'and you build strong!'. He also, it seems, built reliable, for with his second car (still rear-engined) he was the very first Parisian to make the summer drive that is now an annual ritual, from the capital to the coast, covering the 225 km from his works in the Avenue d'Ivry to his summer home at Etretat in a total running time of 23 hours 15 minutes on 31 July/1 August 1891. The greatest annoyance he found was the need to stop every so often and refill the surface carburettor, which also acted as a fuel tank, and only

Right: one of the early Peugeot *vis-à-vis* cars of the early 1890s; chain driven and handlebar steered, these vehicles were Daimler powered and cooling of the rear-mounted V-twin engine was effected by a radiator mounted at the front of the car; the coolant passed through the chassis tubes (Peugeot Collection, France)

Below: René Panhard and Emile Levassor

held 1.3 litres. 'It's true', he philosophised, 'that I made use of the halts to fill up the water tank and grease the car'.

This journey, however, was eclipsed less than two years later when his partner's 23-year-old son, Hippolyte Panhard, set out from the factory bound for Nice, driving the 2 hp car which his father had bought at a specially reduced price of 4318 francs on 28 August 1892, as a present for the young man. Leaving Paris via the Bois de Vincennes, Hippolyte drove the solid-tyred vehicle gingerly over the cobbled quais at Alfort, which had last been paved during the reign of Louis XIV. Once he reached the smoother roads beyond the city, though, he engaged the third speed, and allowed the carriage to reach a heady seventeen kph. 'It's possible to attain twenty kph, but such great speeds require considerable attention on the part of the driver, and are not always advisable', warned the company's catalogue. Pausing for an excellent lunch at Fontaine-bleu, Hippolyte, who was accompanied by his uncle Georges Méric, covered 140 km in the day, noting in a letter to his father that 'some undulations of the terrain often compelled the use of second gear'.

Their progress was also impeded by the fringed canopy attached to the car, which caught the wind, so they abandoned it the next morning. Obtaining fuel was another problem, and they had to search for sources of supply: at Pouilly they were given 23 litres of gasoline by the owner of an 'oil-engined plough', while in another town, Hippolyte had to buy his fuel in a grocer's shop.

'Unfortunately, I had stopped behind the grocer's handcart. As I got down from the car, I pushed the clutch lever and the car jerked forward, overturning the handcart. Cost: 10 francs . . .'

As the car stuttered through villages, it attracted a vast amount of attention. 'Urchins, dogs, cats and chickens all rushed after us, each making their own distinctive noise. It was a dreadful racket . . .'

The important factor was that Hippolyte and Georges Méric were not making a test run: they were touring, and touring in a relatively relaxed manner. 'Yesterday at dinner there were five exquisite courses, much appreciated by Uncle Georges. Dinner, two rooms, stabling for the car and breakfast cost us a total of 10 francs. It's really not expensive . . .'

There were few mechanical annoyances on the road. Descending the steep Col de la République, they free-wheeled, and the car ran 'silently, like running on velvet', but the brakes overheated badly, and Georges Méric had to hold a bucket of water between his legs and cool the brakes with a wet rag. Nearing their destination, the travellers paused at Hyères, where Belhomme, a mechanic from Ivry, replaced Méric. It seems that a few components had dropped from

Above: a famous name in motoring was born in 1886, when the old woodworking machinery firm of Périn and Pauwels passed to René Panhard and Emile Levassor on Périn's death. The earliest Panhard & Levassor cars had their engines either at the rear or in the middle, but by 1893 the partners had established what was to become the classic layout – front engine, central gearbox and rear-wheel drive. This 1892 example, which has a rear-mounted 2¾hp engine, must have been built early in the year, as it is fitted with iron 'tyres' and it was in 1892 that these gave way to solid rubber ones; tiller steering, however, prevailed for several more years

Right: setting the classic pattern for motor vehicles is this 1894 Panhard & Levassor. It has a front-mounted engine, gearbox in the middle and rear-wheel drive

Above: the Honourable Evelyn Hills proudly displays his Panhard & Levassor to a gathering in England in the 1890s

Below: by the mid 1890s, the motor car was becoming an accepted form of reliable transport, as shown by these two young ladies who have ventured out in their 1895 Panhard & Levassor

the car during the eight day run (the French still call spares 'detached pieces'!) and a request for replacements was telegraphed to Levassor.

In Cannes, Nice and Monaco, the Panhard was the centre of attention, and Hippolyte showed it off at the best hotels, theatres, casinos and promenades, in front of prominent personalities.

However, the clutch (which was Levassor's eccentric 'brush' design) was beginning to play up: 'M. Levassor will say that I drove the car very badly, but I assure you that I took every possible care of it and did not try to climb hills more quickly by slipping the clutch'. And there were demonstration runs to be given to important prospective customers... 'a whole heap of Englishmen and the Grand Duke of Mecklembourg, cousin of the Grand Duchess Michael'.

The Grand Duchess Michael was keen to buy a car and drive it herself, and asked Hippolyte to drive her party to the Golf Club of which her husband was president.

'There will be three or four of them', wrote Hippolyte to his father, 'and it seems that they are all big and fat...' The reason for his anxiety was that misbehaving clutch. 'I'll try and put a wedge behind the clutch spring which, by the grace of God, will make it engage better. It would be awful to fail in front of all those grand people.'

The clutch did not fail, luckily, and the car continued to attract attention during Hippolyte's stay at Nice. On the way home, though, the young man tempted fate by driving into the mountains beyond Grasse and, sure enough, the clutch packed up, and the car had to be hauled to the next village behind horses. 'Anyway, it's been a picturesque journey', said Hippolyte philosophically.

It had been a journey, too, which could hardly have been made anywhere else but in France and emphasised that country's lead in the construction and use of motor vehicles.

In America, for instance, the number of successful gasoline carriages which had been built up to that date could be counted on the fingers of one hand, even though George Baldwin Selden had made his first patent application for a 'reliable road locomotive, simple, cheap, lightweight, easy to control and powerful enough to climb any ordinary hill' in 1879, and on the basis of this patent (which was not published until 1895!) attempted to gain a monopoly of the nascent American motor industry.

The first American motor vehicle appears to have been the unsuccessful Schank tricycle exhibited at the 1886 Ohio State Fair. This had an engine 'as big as a kitchen stove', and was chiefly important in having inspired young

5160. MANSION HOUSE & CHEAPSIDE,

Charles Duryea, a cycle manufacturer from Peoria, to start experiments with an 'atmospheric engine'. Curiously enough, American pioneers seem to have almost wilfully ignored the fact that perfectly good power units were readily available to them on a cash and carry basis as early as 1891, when Gottlieb Daimler's friend William Steinway (of piano fame) began building Daimler engines under licence in his Long Island factory, a venture which lasted until 1896.

It seems that the first successful American car was the three-wheeler built by John W. Lambert, of Ohio City, which was running—and photographed—in January or February 1891. The same year, Henry Nadig of Allentown, Pennsylvania, built a four-wheeler vehicle with a single-cylinder power unit, which does not seem to have been too successful, for it was replaced two years later by a twin-cylinder engine, in which form the car was operated until 1903 (it still exists, as does the 1892 Schloemer from Milwaukee).

In September 1893, Charles Duryea and his brother Frank made their first successful trials with a horseless carriage in the streets of Springfield, Massachussets. However, Frank recalled fifty years later 'because of its friction transmission, the car was barely operative, and I was never able to give a demonstration to a prospective client'.

More success and a measure of financial backing were forthcoming eventually, and in 1895 the Duryeas founded America's first motor-manufacturing firm, the Duryea Motor Wagon Company, in Springfield. The following year they set up an agency in London, under the aegis of one J. L. McKim, but this pioneering venture was short-lived.

In any case, Britain was far from being an ideal market for would-be motor magnates: successive Governments had compounded the asininities of the Locomotives on Highways Act to the point of absurdity by insisting that

THE HORSELESS AGE.

DURYEA
MOTOR WAGON
* * COMPANY,
SPRINGFIELD, MASS.
MANUFACTURERS OF
Motor Wagons,
Motors, and * * *
Automobile Vehicles
of all kinds.

Above: advertising for the 1896 Duryea, said to be America's first motor car. Frank Duryea was so impressed with a Benz he saw in 1895 that he based his design on it. In 1896 the Duryeas set up an agency in London but, largely thanks to short-sighted legislation, England was not ready

74

Above: the 1894 Bremer, a Benz-influenced machine built by Frederick W. Bremer, a young engineer from Walthamstow, disputes the title of Britain's first four-wheeled, internal-combustion-engined car with the contemporary Knight

Left: London did not have to wait for the motor car to bring traffic chaos. Save for the motive power, little has changed since this scene at the Mansion House of around 1900

Below: a policeman casts a wary eye over a red-flag bearer in 1895. The Red Flag Act caused many problems for motorists at that time and, judging by the size of the flag, it is a wonder that anyone noticed it

lightweight motor cars should be subject to the same regulations as adipose traction engines, especially with regard to having a crew of two aboard to attend to the mechanism, plus a third to walk ahead to warn of the vehicle's approach. Thus, those who wished to experiment with self-propelled vehicles had to behave like clandestine criminals, and some of the most able, like Edward Butler, of Newbury, who built an ingenious petroleum tricycle in 1888, abandoned their vehicles in disgust. Frederick Bremer, of Walthamstow, a young cycling enthusiast, who had conceived the idea of fitting a gas engine to his cycle during the 1880s, began building a tiny, Benz-inspired car in 1892, which he completed a couple of years later. He ran it very little, and always after dark, to avoid infringing the law, and eventually abandoned it in his garden shed, from which he disinterred it some forty years later and presented it to the local museum. It was restored during the 1960s and successfully completed the London–Brighton Veteran Car Run.

John Henry Knight, of Farnham, Surrey, who had built a steam car in the mid 1860s, and who now owned the Reliance Motor Works, builders of stationary engines, had a three-wheeled car constructed there in 1895; in its later, four-wheeled form, it is now preserved in the National Motor Museum at Beaulieu. Knight was understandably bitter about the anti-motoring attitude of the British Government: 'It is this prejudice which has allowed England to be flooded with French and German motor cars, and the sum of money that has crossed the Channel for the purchase of these cars must have been very considerable', he wrote in 1902. 'Money lost to this country, because our legislators refused to allow motor cars to run on English roads! Had it not been for these restrictions, we might have taken the lead in self-propelled carriages, instead of leaving it to the Germans and French. A lost trade is seldom if ever recovered. French-made cars are now to be found in most foreign countries and our colonies, and we may be sure that these makers will do all they can to keep the trade they have obtained—partly through the want of foresight on the part of our House of Commons.'

Certainly, the manner in which the Daimler patents were handled in Britain in the early 1890s compared very unfavourably with the situation in France. Frederick Richard Simms, a young mechanical engineer from Warwick, had

Above: the 1895 Knight, challenger to the Bremer's claim to be Britain's first petrol-driven road vehicle. John Henry Knight adapted one of his 'Trusty' stationary engines to drive what was originally a three-wheeler, the fourth wheel being added for the 1896 Crystal Palace Motor Show

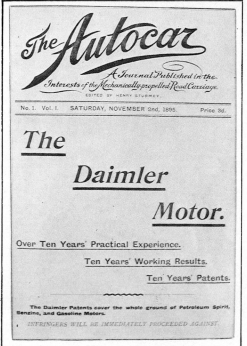

The Autocar

A Journal Published in the Interests of the Mechanically-propelled Road Carriage.

EDITED BY HENRY STURMEY.

No. 1. Vol. I.   SATURDAY, NOVEMBER 2nd, 1895.   Price 3d.

The

Daimler

Motor.

Over Ten Years' Practical Experience.

Ten Years' Working Results.

Ten Years' Patents.

The Daimler Patents cover the whole ground of Petroleum Spirit, Benzine, and Gasoline Motors.

INFRINGERS WILL BE IMMEDIATELY PROCEEDED AGAINST.

Above right: an example of the first Daimler to be built in Great Britain; a two-cylinder machine, it was constructed on contemporary Panhard lines and had a four-speed-plus-reverse transmission. Prices ranged from about £360 to £420

Left: even as early as 1895, Daimler could advertise 'Over Ten Years Practical Experience' on the cover of the very first edition of *The Autocar*. Over eighty years later, the magazine still survives

met Gottlieb Daimler at an exhibition in Germany at the end of the 1880s, and had acquired the Daimler rights for the United Kingdom and its colonies (except Canada). However, he found it difficult to popularise this power unit, due to the restrictive laws which dissuaded most people from attempting to go motoring. So, the first public demonstration of the Daimler engine in Britain took place in 1891 with a motor launch brought to London from Cannstatt, with which trials took place on the Thames at Putney.

Nevertheless, Simms formed the Daimler Motor Syndicate Limited, to handle Daimler products, and an arch was rented at Putney Bridge Railway Station, where the Syndicate's main activity consisted of converting launches to petrol power (around this time three young brothers called Lanchester were also experimenting with a petrol launch powered by their own engine).

In 1895, Simms imported the first Cannstatt-Daimler car to be seen in Britain, and was approached by a syndicate which saw the possibility of vast profits in the new invention, and were willing to pay a considerable sum of money to acquire the Daimler rights. Prominent in this syndicate was Harry J. Lawson, an engineer turned company promoter. He had received his training in raising large amounts of cash for dubious projects during the bicycle boom

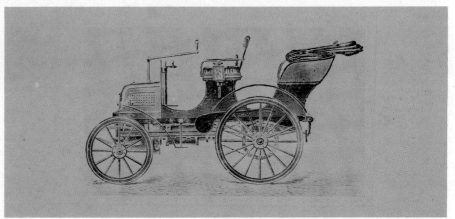

of the early 1890s at the hand of the notorious Terah Hooley, whose name had become synonymous with the securing of capital for companies whose potential never quite managed to match the glowing terms of the share prospectus.

Lawson's training as a cycle engineer, and his experience of the cycle boom, convinced him that once the law with regard to motor vehicles was relaxed, a similar boom in self-propelled transportation could occur, and he intended to be the one to profit from such a situation. To which end, he set about systematically acquiring the British rights to all the leading Continental patents (although he also acquired a considerable amount of costly dross along the way), and then launched a manufacturing group to exploit them.

In January 1896, he floated the Daimler Motor Company, and set about publicising the 'new locomotion', especially through the columns of *The Autocar*, one of the very first motoring journals, which had been founded in November 1895 as the mouthpiece of the Lawson organisation (and which was to prove infinitely more durable than its sponsor).

By continued lobbyings, Lawson persuaded Parliament to change its attitude to the motor car (the Marquis of Salisbury, whose Conservative administration was then in power, subsequently became a keen motorist himself) and to bring in a new Act which freed motor carriages weighing less than three tons from the need to carry two people, and abolished the peripatetic harbinger altogether, raising the overall speed limit to 12 mph.

To commemorate the 'throwing open of the highways', Lawson organised a run from London to Brighton, on 14 November 1896—'Emancipation Day'.

The administration of the event was maybe a little dubious—at least one of the vehicles which reached Brighton did so by courtesy of the Southern Railway Company—but at least Britain was now on the way to being a country with its own indigenous motor-manufacturing industry, and could begin to make up the ground which had been lost to it by the Law.

CHAPTER 5

The Veteran Years of Motoring

Left: an 1898 Decauville *Voiturelle* built by a French railway locomotive firm. This vehicle featured sliding-pillar front suspension, although the designer has ignored any springing at the rear. As with most vehicles of this type and age, the manufacturers went to De Dion for their power units, in this case a twin-cylinder unit of 489 cc

'What is it?
'It is an Autocar.
'Some people call it a motor car.
'It is worked by a petroleum motor.
'The motor is of four horsepower.
'It will run sixty miles with one charge of oil.
'No! It can't explode – there is no boiler.
'It can travel at 14 mph.
'Ten to eleven is its average pace.
'It can be started in two minutes.
'There are eight ways of stopping it so it can't run away.
'It is steered with one hand.
'Speed is mainly controlled by the foot.
'It can be stopped in ten feet when travelling at full speed.
'It carries four gallons of oil and sixteen gallons of water.
'The water is to keep the engine cool.
'It costs less than three-farthings a mile to run.
'The car can carry five people.
'It can get up any ordinary hill.
'It was built by the Daimler Motor Company of Coventry and cost £370.
'We have come from John O'Groats House.
'We are going to Land's End.
'We are not record-breaking but touring for pleasure.'

These words, printed on little cards which were handed out to members of the public along the road from John O'Groats to Land's End, were the bare facts behind the first epic drive on British soil. It was, after all, less than a year since 'Emancipation Day', and the infant British motor industry had done little except relieve credulous investors of a considerable amount of money. Indeed, when Henry Sturmey, founding editor of *The Autocar*, set out on this marathon drive in his newly delivered Daimler on 2 October 1897, the Daimler company had been building cars for only a few months. During 1896 and most of 1897, they had been importing Daimler and Panhard cars from the continent, and their first production models were, indeed, straight copies of the contemporary Panhard. They constructed the frames and engines. Their associates, the Motor Manufacturing Company, produced the carriagework, and it was a toss-up whether the finished vehicle was sold as a Daimler or an MMC.

Sturmey's long drive, on which he covered a total of 1600 miles, and took seventeen days (including three days' rest) to cover the 939 miles from furthest north to furthest south, showed the basic reliability of the design. He had no trouble apart from clutch slip brought on by a howling gale which drenched the entire car, its occupants and its mechanism, and the total failure of the inadequate braking system on the descent of the Kirkstone Pass. The car ran away, attaining the suicidal velocity of 30 mph, Sturmey avoiding disaster by sitting tight and steering like a demon. He rammed a bank when the car attempted to repeat the episode a few miles further on!

However, not all the pioneers enjoyed such little trouble – after all, Sturmey was a director of the Daimler Company, and his car had doubtless been assembled with more care than a less-exalted order would have received. Among those who suffered from the awkward temperament of the early tube-ignited motor cars was the author Rudyard Kipling, who in a letter written in 1904 looked back over his motoring experiences with wry amusement. 'I like motoring because I have suffered for its sake. I began seven years ago in the days of tube ignition, when 6 hp was reckoned fair allowance for a touring car, and fifteen miles an hour was something to lk about. My agonies, shames, delays, rages, chills, parboilings, road-walkings, water-drawings, burns and starvations – at which you laughed – all went to make your car today safe and comfortable. If there were no dogs there would be no vivisection, and people would still be treated on the lines of Galen and Avicenna. Any fool can invent anything, as any fool can wait to buy the invention when it is thoroughly perfected, but the men to reverence, to admire, to write odes and erect statues to,

are those Prometheuses and Ixions (maniacs, you used to call us) who chase the inchoate idea to fixity up and down the King's Highway with their red right shoulders to the wheel . . .'

However, it was not just mechanically that the pioneers suffered. Harry Lawson's house-of-cards empire started running into trouble within two years of its inception. Most of the components of that empire were housed in the Motor Mills, a converted four-storey cotton-mill building on a thirteen-acre site near the Coventry Canal, which had been acquired in 1896 (and advertised as 'the largest autocar factory in the world . . . for the manufacture of autocars under the Pennington, Daimler and Bollée systems . . . 200 highly skilled workmen' before the Lawson companies had even moved in!). Here at various times were housed Daimler, the Motor Manufacturing Company, the Great Horseless Carriage Company, Humber & Company, the British Motor Syndicate, the Beeston Pneumatic Tyre Company, the Coventry Motor Company . . .

Above: based on the original Renault, this 1899 car has a slightly longer wheelbase than that machine and is powered by an air-cooled 1¾ hp De Dion engine, driving the rear wheels via a three-speed gearbox, propeller shaft and differential
(Skokloster Museum, Sweden)

Right: a Delahaye *vis-a-vis* of 1898, again, a fairly conventional design of small car, with a rear-mounted 'slow-running' engine (Château de Grandson, Switzerland)

Below: an example of original thinking in the motor-car world is shown by this 1898 Egg. The car, which was built in Zurich, features variable-ratio belt transmission, which was later to appear in the DAF cars of the 1950s (Château de Grandson, Switzerland)

These companies lived, for the most part, a curiously incestuous existence, robbing Peter to pay Paul by complex financial double-shuffles like the 1898 acquisition of the Great Horseless Carriage Company by the British Motor Syndicate, where some £300,000 did a now-you-see-it-now-you-don't vanishing trick to, it seems, the complete satisfaction of 4000 out of 4070 shareholders who did not realise they had been comprehensively gulled . . .

The British Motor Syndicate, indeed, does not appear to have actually *built* anything. True, it issued some very handsome brochures, although half the vehicles in these were total improbabilities and the other half consisted of imported Panhards (which, Lawson generously conceded, with somewhat less than a regard for the truth, had been 'built under British Motor Syndicate Patents'). It did, however, rigorously pursue those hapless individuals who were presumed to have trespassed against those expensively bought patents.

Take the case of the would-be motor manufacturer from Birmingham against whom the Syndicate took action in 1896. 'An order was immediately made restraining the defendant from proceeding further with the infringement, and a wholesale order was made for the destruction of the parts produced'.

Right: a busy scene at the Daimler factory in 1900, with a whole range of cars in various stages of completion. It all looks rather haphazard and, indeed, it must have been difficult working out which car was where. Henry Ford was later to make things easier with his mass-production techniques

Below: Gottlieb Daimler is acknowledged as the father of the petrol engine. Daimler's early research culminated in his first high-speed engine in 1883 and his first purpose built car in 1889. His early cars were the basis for a multitude of copies throughout the world. The car below was built in 1899, the year in which Daimler introduced his first four-cylinder engine (National Motor Museum, England)

Below: a scene in Billancourt in 1898; Marcel Renault, on the left, is in the front of a contemporary quadricycle, his brother, Louis, is at the wheel of the car in the centre and Paul Huge is in the prototype Renault. The Renault's power unit is a De Dion 273cc, air-cooled, $1\frac{3}{4}$ hp engine, driving through a three-speed-and-reverse gearbox. In the first six months, the Renaults sold over sixty cars

Added Lawson, casually: 'I am sorry to say that the man committed suicide . . . in the circumstances, and on representation being made to me, the directors accepted £150 instead of £600, due under one head of the infringement . . . The case proved that the patents are the absolute property of the Syndicate, and as much property as freehold land'.

This, when the Syndicate was little more than a squatter on the freehold of other men's ideas, was rankest hypocrisy. However, one gets the impression that Lawson was so puffed up with vanity that he could not see the dubiousness of the premises from which he was arguing. His father had been a Methodist minister, and it seems as though Lawson regarded himself as a prophet sent to lead the faithful into the promised land flowing, if not with milk and honey, at least with unlimited share capital.

For all his ridiculous posturings and grandiose schemes, Lawson did attract some able men into his organisation, among the charlatans like E. J. Pennington, the American inventor who matched Harry J. at his own game by selling him the rights to some pretty amazing vehicles, none of which was capable of running more than a short distance without mishap.

Among the gems in Lawson's dross were a young man named Percival Perry, who was later to head the Ford organisation in Europe, and a brilliant electrical engineer, Walter C. Bersey, who had built an electrical omnibus as early as 1888, while he was still in his teens.

Silent and elegant, Bersey's electric carriages caused a great sensation in London (where, indeed, he was issued with the last summons under the old Locomotives on Highways Act). In 1896, a correspondent from the *East Anglian Daily Times* was a passenger on one of Bersey's many demonstration runs. 'Observing a crowd assembled by the Northumberland Avenue entrance of the Grand Hotel, our correspondent found that it was occasioned by a very smart yellow-wheeled Landau, driven by a gentleman whom he afterwards found to be the inventor of the carriage, which it appeared was owned by the Great Horseless Carriage Company . . . our correspondent was at once

recognised and invited to take a seat . . . The carriage, therefore, amidst a dense crowd which had already assembled, started with a living freight of no less than seven persons, who anticipated that their driver would take them along the less frequented Thames Embankment. On the contrary, the intrepid Mr Bersey sharply turned round, and with *coeur leger* dashed into the thick of the Strand traffic and into the thick of the light badinage in which the London bus man and cabby are so gifted and fluent.

'Onward we sped, amid cries of "A penny all the way", "Whip behind" and "Where's your 'osses?" – and very instructive it was to observe the sudden surprise of the foot passengers as they realised that the handsome carriage which whisked past them was propelled silently and swiftly without the aid of the patient, nervous, skating quadrupeds to which they were accustomed. As we sped past them, we could easily have thrown one of the early Christmas oranges which were offered us into the gaping mouths of the startled foot passengers.

'Instructive was it to see the problems which the jealous Jehus set our driver by pulling their clumsy buses and cabs across his path, but calm and unmoved our skilful coachman brought his obedient motor carriage to rest within a few inches of the adversary, and when they gave him the slightest chance, flew, without apparent movement, swiftly and resistlessly past every vehicle, all the while having his machine under absolute control.

'Our correspondent, having no business instincts, had no thought beyond the absolute comfort of being propelled with the touch of the tiny lever at will, without effort, and without work or suffering to dumb, patient animals, wheresoever he wills. In his mind's eye, he beholds the streets of the 20th Century free from the crack of the cruel whip, the struggles of terrified animals, with traffic swiftly and silently passing through comely and cleanly streets, emancipated from the tyranny of the merciless "friends of the horse" . . . To show the docility of the electric carriage of towns, our driver assured us he had driven his chairman (the Earl of Winchelsea) and six other directors of the Great Horseless Carriage Company, from Westminster to Ludgate Circus and back (eight miles), through the thick of the Strand traffic, in thirty minutes. Welcome the motor car!'

Certainly, in the early days of motoring, it was the electric car which appealed most to the non-motoring classes. Bersey, who had invented a new type of dry battery which promised a longer service life than the lead-acid type, was obviously convinced that the electric vehicle was superior to its rivals, as he told the *Gentleman's Journal* in 1896: 'The petroleum motor carriage inevitably subjects its occupants to annoyances from which its electric rival is entirely free. The former is subject to excessive vibration, smell, noise and heat. From all these defects the electric car is free. Moreover, the petroleum motor requires an engineer to drive it, that is, if the danger of explosion is to be reduced to a minimum. The electric car is so simple that any coachman may learn to manipulate it in less than half-an-hour!'.

However, although Bersey attempted to popularise the electric by operating a fleet of cabs on the streets of London, the venture was short-lived. Right from the beginning, the major drawbacks which have always bedevilled the electric vehicle were apparent: the cabs could run no more than fifty miles on one charge, and then had to return to a generating station, either to take on fresh batteries (which weighed fourteen cwt!) or to be recharged (which took several hours), and, when the batteries reached the end of their service life, replacements were costly. With this constant need to return to base, no wonder that Americans nicknamed electric vehicles 'homing pigeons'!

The failure of the London Electrical Cab Company was one of the first cracks to appear in the elaborate corporate set-up of the Lawson organisation. Once one component had collapsed, however, the rest were not far behind; it was the affair of the Electric Tramways Construction and Maintenance Company which was to prove Lawson's ultimate downfall. In this instance, Lawson was acting as nominee for his old mentor, Terah Hooley, who, as an undischarged bankrupt, was debarred from trading. This company attracted official attention, however, with the result that Lawson and Hooley were

Not looking that much more advanced than the
Viktoria and the Velo is this Benz Comfortable
of 1898

Left: the single-cylinder Dumont's novel transmission used revolving steel discs on each end of the transverse crankshaft, across the faces of which moved friction discs connected to the rear wheels through shafts and bevel gears (Château de Grandson, Switzerland)

Below: the 1000-Miles Trial was contested by 65 cars, representing most of the leading manufacturers of the day. Here the Hon C. S. Rolls and S. F. Edge contemplate Edge's 8 hp Napier. Edge was the company's first distributor and the 8 hp was their first complete car. It featured a front-mounted, 2.4-litre, twin-cylinder engine, four-speed gearbox and chain drive

manufacturers. Other British car makers represented were Wolseley (makers of sheep-shearing machinery, whose chief engineer, Herbert Austin, was investigating the possibilities of motor-car manufacture) and Lanchester. There was, too, a representative cross-section of imported models: Panhards and De Dions from France, Benz and Orient Express cars from Germany, Locomobile and Brown-Whitney steamers from America.

The crowds who turned out to watch the event more than met the organising club's expectations. 'In the cities and towns, the footpaths and roads have been so densely crowded with spectators that only the narrowest passage remained through which the motor vehicles had to pass. At every cross road in the country there were knots of on-lookers from the neighbouring villages, the parson and his daughters on bicycles, the country squire on his horse, the old dowager safely ensconsed in her landau, coaching parties enjoying champagne lunches at the road side, and cyclists in legions. In villages, the children were given a "whole holiday", and were ranged on the school walls and cheered each motor as it passed. The confidence of the spectators in the control of their vehicles was, although flattering, decidedly embarrassing, for the crowds assembled at the bottoms of hills left a lane of barely seven-feet wide through which the vehicles had to pass at high speed. The police seemed to share with the public a keen enjoyment in seeing vehicles at thirty miles an hour, and sympathised with the rebukes which the crowd addressed to drivers who failed to go at top speed. Generally, the public looked on the passage of the motors as they do the passage of a fire-engine, namely, as a fine inspiring sight which makes the pulse beat faster and satisfies a craving for excitement.'

castle control. Towing or pushing would, with most people, have been an easy(?) solution to the difficulty, but Mr Grahame-White would have none of either, and determined to steer the vehicle with his foot, which he successfully accomplished by standing on the offside step, guiding the wheels with the hollow of his right foot on to the outside axle box, and thus wise did he travel right through to Newcastle, making his average speed for the day ten miles per hour. The only person who seemed to think nothing of the feat was Mr Grahame-White.'

Difficulties of quite a different kind were experienced by the journalist A. J. Wilson, who wrote for the cycling press under the pseudonym 'Faed' (he was stone deaf, and merely spelt his disability backwards as a penname). Much of the power of his Ariel tricycle was lost through an improperly closed compression tap. He could not hear the tell-tale hissing that indicated this fault, and just pedalled harder on hills to supplement what seemed to be a particularly unenthusiastic engine. He must have had legs like piston-rods, for the *Automotor Journal* reported: 'The time of Mr A. J. Wilson on his Ariel for Taddington Hill is remarkable, but it must be borne in mind that Mr Wilson's skill in pedalling is a factor in the case, which an ordinary flabby mortal under like conditions would have to allow for. When the longer hills had to be negotiated, Mr. Wilson's state of collapse was a thing to be seen, and not easily forgotten'.

For the record, Wilson pedalled up Taddington at an average speed of 18.91mph, compared with Rolls's Panhard, which achieved 17.77mph under full power . . .

Eventually, the competitors returned to London, and the Thousand Miles' Trial was brought to a successful conclusion. Then, as now, some manufacturers treated a minor class win as the occasion for vast, shrieking headlines in the motor press, a trend which offended the *Automotor Journal*: 'The public will be induced, by misleading assertions, to purchase vehicles which will disgust them once and for all with automobilism. The natural argument will be that if this is the sort of car that was able to be "first everywhere", a day spent in assisting an itinerant knife grinder now and again by way of relaxation would be equally exhilarating and less expensive'.

The Trial had done immense good in promoting goodwill for the motor car throughout England, although a few entrenched diehards still fulminated against it. At least one bastion of the Law was a staunch automobilist, though – Lord Kingsburgh, the Lord Justice Advocate of Scotland, who was a passenger in one of the competing cars. Summing up the achievements of the Trial, he concluded: 'One of these vehicles, going twelve to fourteen miles an hour, could be absolutely pulled up in less than its own length. That was an element of safety unattainable with horses . . . there have been several breakdowns, and some cars have been dropped, but in almost every case – indeed, in every case – the fault was not with the motor machinery, but because the coachbuilder had not understood the proper strength of wheels or axles or springs to provide for such vehicles. Automobilism, in my opinion, is not only a sport, but provision for locomotion in this country which is needed and will be efficient'.

If in England motoring was just beginning to throw off the shadow of the Lawsonian era, American manufacturers were now faced with a far more pernicious patent monopoly, which was to create news, not only in the motoring world, for a long time to come.

George Baldwin Selden, having neatly bided his time until the first experimental cars were running on American roads, published his 1879 patent in 1895, and then claimed that all gasoline-driven vehicles developed since 1879 were infringements of that patent. He had not, let it be added, actually built a car to prove that his invention was practicable, although he had at one stage attempted to raise the capital to do so, only to frighten off the potential investor with the remark: 'Jim, you and I will live to see more carriages on Main Street run by motors than are now drawn by horses'.

However, the delay had proved fortuitous for Selden. By waiting until 1895, he had gained the maximum effective life for his patent, although at first he

lacked the money to enforce it. In 1899, he began negotiations to raise the necessary capital, and was on the point of closing negotiations with five Wall Street bankers who were prepared to put up $250,000 when fate – and a gullible patent attorney named Herman Cuntz – stuck a far bigger fish on his hook, in the shape of the Pope Manufacturing Company, America's leading cycle manufacturer. They were considering going into car manufacture, and asked Cuntz to investigate any patents which might affect this multi-million-dollar venture. He had already come across the Selden patent, and attempted to proclaim its merits to his employers . . . whose engineering experts dismissed it at once. But ex-Navy Secretary William Whitney, head of the consortium which was providing the capital for the Pope venture, proved a more receptive audience for Cuntz and, on learning that Selden would rather his patent be administered by a car company than by investors, decided to make a deal, and took an option on Selden's patent until January 1900, in which the Pope-Whitney interests were given a 'definitive licence' – in effect an assignment of the patent – in exchange for $10,000 plus a percentage of any royalties collected.

The patent's validity having been attested by a British 'expert' named Dugald Clerk (who, although he knew a great deal about two-stroke gas engines, was far from being an authority on motor cars), the Pope-Whitney group – the Columbia and Electric Vehicle Company – was reformed as an $18,000,000 corporation, the Electric Vehicle Company, and set about prosecuting the manufacturers who were, in all innocence, transgressing against Selden's patent.

With its vast finances, the Electric Vehicle Company had little difficulty in steam-rolling the token resistance put up by most American manufacturers into the ground, and by September 1902 the motor manufacturers were ready to negotiate. An Association of Licenced Automobile Manufacturers was set up,

Above: there are few more famous names in the history of motoring than that of Henry Ford. Ford's vast manufacturing operation is based on a background of inspired innovation which was Henry's best known personal characteristic. The company began operations, shakily at first, in 1903 and by the end of that year they were firmly established. Ford himself died in 1947, aged 84, but the company carries on to the present with a strong family involvement

Above: the 1901 Oldsmobile Curved Dash is regarded as the world's first mass-production car. It had a single-cylinder, 1.6-litre engine and chain-drive. In 1903, Whitman and Hammond drove a Curved Dash from San Francisco to New York
(Château de Grandson, Switzerland)

Left: A 1901 Rochet-Schneider. The French company had a tendency to copy other manufacturers' designs, the model here being a Panhard type, but made up for a lack of originality by sound engineering.
(Château de Grandson, Switzerland)

which paid 2/5 of 2.5 per cent of the retail price of each car to the EVC, retained 2/5 of that amount for its own coffers, and paid the remaining 1/5 to Selden (who seems to have paid half his share to the manager of the ALAM!). Not all the Association's concerns were monetary, however, for it made a genuine attempt to create uniform standards throughout the motor industry, establishing standard sizes for screw threads, copper and steel tubes, and many other common fittings. Moreover, association members could obtain access to all the latest technical information free of charge, enjoyed a standardised system of contracts, guarantees and agreements, and had their products featured in the ALAM's annual *Handbook of Gasolene Automobiles*, which claimed that 'each manufacturer or importer conducts his business entirely independent of the other and, of course, in open competition' (although the ALAM also seems to have existed as a price-fixing ring). Customers were assured, too, that buying a car manufactured under the Selden Patent was a 'guarantee . . . that secures to the purchaser freedom from the annoyance and expense of litigation because of infringement of this patent'.

However, as ALAM also chose who could be licensed, its activities represented a brake on free enterprise, and Henry Ford (who had founded the Ford Motor Company in the summer of 1903 after a couple of false starts) decided that it had nothing to offer him. His aim, after all, was to produce a $500 motor car which anyone could afford, and the average price of ALAM-built cars was $1382.

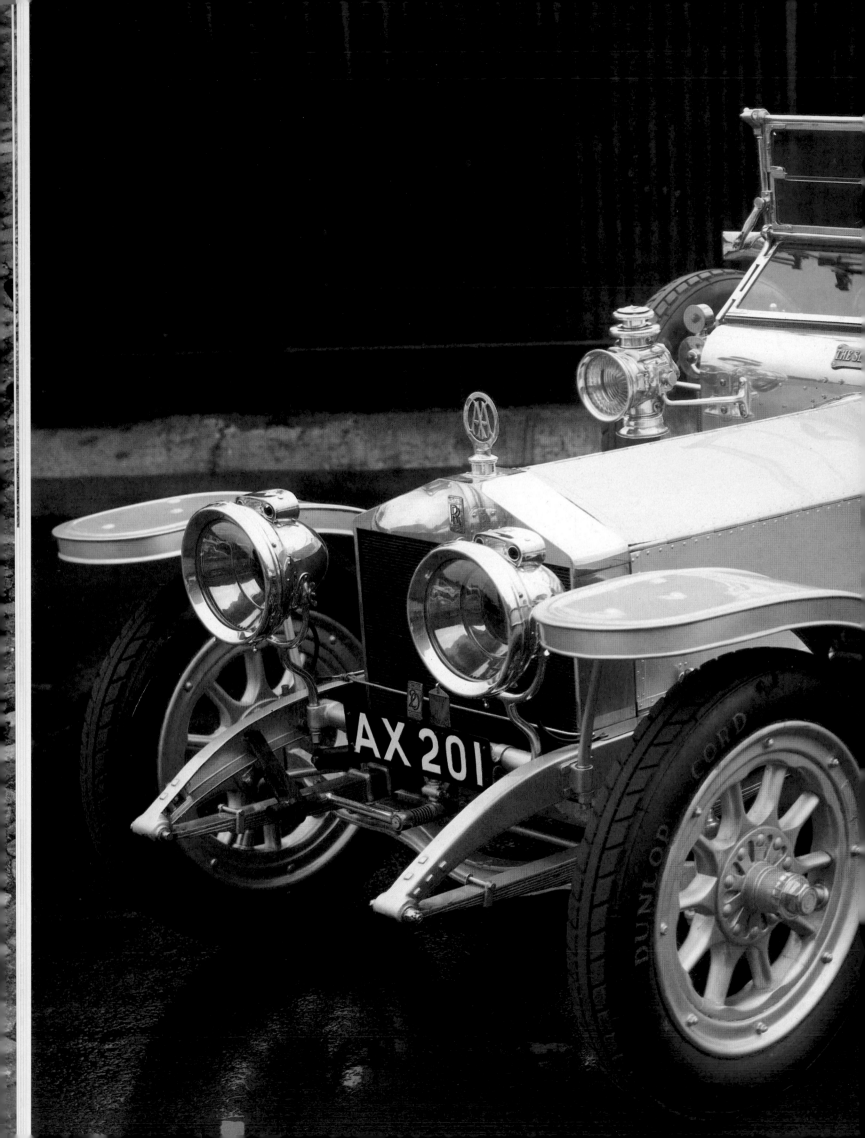

offer from Mr Rolls to try a similar two-cylinder car then and there on the Champs-Elysees. It was, in a single word, a revelation . . . Never before had I been in a car which made so little noise, vibrated so little, ran so smoothly, or could be turned about so easily and readily in a maze of traffic. Indeed, the conclusion that I almost reached there and then was that the car was too silent and ghostlike to be safe . . . When, wandering again through the Grand Palais in 1906, I came across a six-cylinder Rolls-Royce in one of the galleries, the extraordinary measure of progress which had been achieved in the interval, and the shortness of the interval, came upon me in a flash, and struck me "all of a heap", as the saying goes'.

In 1906, the 30 hp Rolls-Royce six-cylinder model defeated a four-cylinder Martini in a reliability trial which received the popular title 'the Battle of the Cylinders'.

Shortly afterwards, J. E. Vincent drove from London to Norfolk in the victorious Rolls-Royce: 'There was no reason in life against a good spin at top speed except that superstitious regard for the letter of the law which not one man in a thousand really has. The car simply flew forward; the speed indicator

marked 25, 30, 35, 40, 45 and even 50 miles an hour; the road seemed to open wide to our advent, to stretch out its arms, so to speak, to embrace us; the motion, smooth, swifter and swifter still, even as the flight of the albatross, that stirreth not his wings, and absolutely free from vibration, was, in a single word divine'.

Yet the 30 hp Rolls-Royce was supposed not to have been a particularly successful model . . . In fact, after only half-a-dozen had been produced, the 30 hp was replaced by the illustrious 40/50 hp six, which was soon christened the 'Silver Ghost' after the most famous of the early examples produced, which in 1907 was subjected to a 15,000 mile trial by the RAC. It had already travelled from Bexhill, in Sussex, to Edinburgh and Glasgow, using only direct-drive third gear and overdrive top, at an average fuel consumption of 20.8 mpg!

On the sixth day of the 15,000-mile test, a petrol tap vibrated shut, bringing the Silver Ghost to its only involuntary stop (apart from tyre trouble) of the entire run. At the end of the 15,000 miles, the RAC officials stripped down the car to see which parts, in their opinion, should be renewed in order to return the Rolls-Royce to 'as-new' condition: 'The engine was passed as perfect; the transmission throughout was passed as perfect; one or two parts of the steering details showed very slight wear, perhaps one-thousandth part of an inch, and the committee condemned these as not being "as good as new"; they also required the small universal joints in the magneto drive to be replaced, and the water-pump to be repacked; and this was all that was required for making the car equal to new after a mileage which many cars do not cover in three years' work'.

Some of the credit, however, should be given to the car's mechanics and

Above left: this 1903 Spyker racer was the world's first six-cylinder car. The 8.7-litre engine drove all four wheels and each wheel was braked. Although the six-cylinder racing car was never put into series production, several 32/40 hp four-cylinder examples, with four-wheel-drive and four-wheel-brakes, were built

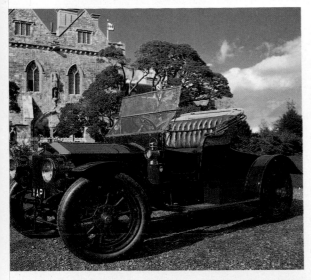

chauffeur, for during the trial, it spent 40 hours 'in the motor houses . . . for repairs, replacements, and adjustments'. Concluded the RAC: 'The running of the car was excellent, except for a slight tendency to misfiring at low speeds during a part of the trial. The car (as a whole) and the engine (in particular) were exceptionally quiet (especially on the third speed, direct drive) and free from vibration. The springs, however, at the back of the car were scarcely stiff enough for the load carried. The front footboards became uncomfortably warm'.

The results of the Trial proved the built-in durability of the 40/50 hp Rolls-Royce (due mainly to Henry Royce's early training as a locomotive engineer), and established this well-constructed, if scarcely innovative, car as a claimant for the coveted title of 'The Best Car in the World'.

But the Rolls-Royce hadn't started the six-cylinder trend; that honour belonged to the British Napier company. Although Spyker in Holland and Automotrice in France had constructed six-cylinder cars before Napier, it was the British firm which had established the configuration as a production model, thanks to the remarkable selling powers of Selwyn Francis Edge. As a motoring

Above: three views of a 1907 Napier 60 hp, built as a replica of the car with which S. F. Edge averaged 65.91 mph for 24 hours at Brooklands in that year. The engine is 'square' with 127 mm × 127 mm bore and stroke; this, in six cylinders, gives a displacement of 7724 cc (National Motor Museum, England)

calculated to carry a man to the highest place with the automobile movement'. writer with the pen name 'Auriga' noted in 1907: 'Mr S. F. Edge has shown, indeed, a rare and almost unique combination of the abilities, mental and physical, and of the spirit of enterprise tempered by prudence, which is exactly

'Auriga', apparently, had ridden on one of the very first Napier sixes in 1904 (the first, built in 1903, was sold to a Mr W. Bramson . . . his purchase was 'rather a brave thing to do', thought Edge) and noted: 'A good six-cylinder car is perceptibly and unmistakably more comfortable, more luxurious, less vibrant, less noisy than the best four-cylinder car that ever was built. Some say she ought not to be; but the fact remains that she is and she can be built to what power one pleases. She is easy on tyres, too, and as for her petrol consumption, I am afraid it does not worry me. It is the sort of thing which troubles an omnibus company desirous of making a profit, but it does not cause any anxiety to the rich men and women, of whom the supply is seemingly unlimited, who buy Napier six-cylinder cars. To such people also the argument that the extra luxury is not worth the extra money has no meaning. Like the difference between first and third classes in a railway train, it is worth buying for people who like comfort, and there are many to whom the cost is a matter of no moment'.

At first, though, there seem to have been other considerations than luxury, as Edge recalled over twenty years later: 'I read a paper at the RAC on the advantages of six cylinders over four, and I remember Rolls said that one of the advantages was, you had six strings to your bow instead of four, which rather goes to show the kind of straws we clung to in the early days of motoring. What was in Rolls's mind was that you were more likely to have one cylinder left firing if you had six of them than if you had only four!'.

Right: A 1902 CGV (Charron, Girardot et Voigt) 3.3-litre. After 1906, the cars were called simply Charrons

His was an even more exotic vehicle. Like the Panhard Pullman, it was furnished throughout by the Paris branch of Maple & Company. The centre portion of the body resembled a stagecoach, and once again featured silk chairs which could be turned into a bed. Between the seats were sliding doors leading to the rear of the body, which housed a fully equipped kitchen, in which the Baron's corpulent chef, Emile, cooked meals for his master *en route*.

However, the most remarkable feature of Von Eckhardstein's car, which was reputed to have cost £4000 (or £3300 more than the standard 35 hp De Dietrich on which it was based), was its chassis, which had six wheels, with the front and rear axles steering, and the central axle drove. This curious layout, which also incorporated an unorthodox disposition of the springs, was the invention of a military engineer named Lindecker, who had persuaded De Dietrich to take it up around 1905. It was supposed to soak up all the unevenness of the road, enable the vehicle to run smoothly over potholes and hump-backed bridges, with 'comfort, sweet running, positive steering and safety'.

The Baron had wagered de Castellane that the De Dietrich would 'knock the feathers out of his blasted cocked hat at the Concours', but in fact both cars won high awards.

Perhaps the most consistent of all the concours set was the wealthy Englishman Montague Grahame-White (the same man who had steered his Daimler in the Thousand Miles' Trial by kicking the hub after the steering had broken, and whose brother, Claude, was the most famous British aviator of the day). Grahame-White loved big motor cars, and loved nothing better than to take an already huge vehicle and make it even more eye-catching by lengthening the wheelbase to absurd proportions.

In 1911 Grahame-White owned the biggest of all the pre-war Mercédès, the six-cylinder 75/105 hp model, of 10,179 cc. This was a chain-driven behemoth with canework panelling round the top of its tourer body. Fitted spanners were concealed in the hinged upholstery of the doors and plate glass panels in the top and sides of the bonnet displayed the gun-barrel finish of the cylinder blocks and the highly burnished pipework. A spectacular enough machine, you might think, but it was not enough for Grahame-White. In December 1911 the Mercédès was returned to the coachbuilders, who lengthened the wheelbase to 15 ft 6 in, fitted an aggressively pointed radiator of special design, giant Rushmore acetylene headlamps and new mudwings.

'Monty' was still creating such vehicles during the 1920s; but most of them had long since vanished. Let the epitaph of the Edwardian monsters be Grahame-White cruising down the long, straight avenues of poplars in Burgundy at a steady 90 kilometres an hour on his way to Monte Carlo, pausing only to sample the superb cuisine and the occasional bottle of Chateau Mouton Rothschild '99 – 'no more costly than a Beaujolais in many West End London hotels before the 1914 war'.

Left: Le Zèbre of Puteaux, Seine, built cars between 1909 and 1932; their first cars, like this 1909 model, were powered by 5 hp, 600 cc engines, driving the rear wheels through a two-speed gearbox and a shaft (Château de Grandson, Switzerland)

Right : A Ford Model N, built in 1906 to undercut a similar Oldsmobile; this was the direct predecessor of the Model T (Château de Grandson, Switzerland)

Left : the car with which Ford brought motoring to the masses; the Model T came in many guises from sporty roadster to delivery truck or tractor and, at least between 1914 and 1925, in 'any colour so long as it's black'. This is a 1913 four-seat open tourer. The 'T' used a 2.9-litre, four-cylinder, side-valve engine and pedal-controlled, two-speed transmission. In an eighteen-year production run, over fifteen million Model Ts were built (Hendy-Lennox, Bournemouth)

Although the Sizaire enjoyed several years of popularity and even achieved a number of sporting successes, its formula was obviously a sterile one, for, having reduced a vehicle to the absolute basics, its designers could only elaborate it as customers demanded extra refinement; and the Sizaire-Naudin would end up as a staid – and rather corpulent – light car of conventional design.

What then was the answer to the problem of designing a car for the masses? Already Henry Ford was practising the economies of scale, by raising production and reducing prices. In 1906, for example, he replaced the old Model F, with its twin-cylinder engine beneath the seat, with the four cylinder Model N, a far more sophisticated machine. Model F had cost $1000; Model N was only $600 ('It carries no equipment, it is "just automobile – all automobile"', announced the company) and was exported to Britain where it sold for around £125, a price which caused the deepest suspicion among the home industry. 'Nothing so cheap can be any good,' they said . . . and were duly surprised by the model's success, with annual British sales of 600. Ford, however, had even greater things in mind . . .

'The automobile of the past,' said Ford at that time, 'attained success in spite of its price because there were more than enough purchasers to take the limited output of the then new industry. Proportionately few could buy, but those few could keep all the manufacturers busy, and price, therefore, had no bearing on sales. The automobile of the present is making good because the price has been reduced just enough to add sufficient new purchasers to take care of the increased output. Supply and demand, not cost, has regulated the selling price of automobiles.

'The automobile of the future must be enough better than the present car to beget confidence in the man of limited means and enough lower in price to insure sales for the enormously increased output. The car of the future, "the car for the people", the car that any man can own, who can afford a horse and carriage, is coming sooner than most people expect.

'A limited number of factories can supply all the demand for high-priced cars, but the market for a low-priced car is unlimited. The car of the future will be light as well as low in price. This means the substitution of quality for quantity, even to the use of materials not yet discovered'.

Sometime early in 1907, Ford began development of his own personal vision of that 'car for the people'; already, despite the relatively high price of automobiles, America was becoming a nation of car-owners at a spectacular rate. In 1902 there had been one car to every 1,500,000 citizens of the USA; by 1905 the proportion was one to every 65,000, and in the spring of 1907, one American in 800 owned a car. Now Ford was after the remaining 799.

In the little experimental room, only 12 ft by 15 ft, at Ford's Picquette Avenue plant (which the company had occupied for only a couple of years, yet was already outgrowing) Henry Ford and his associates, C. H. Wills, C. J. Smith and Joseph Galamb were working on the successor to Model N. Models R and

S had been de luxe versions of the N, so the new car was to be called the 'Model T'.

Joseph Galamb, a young Hungarian engineer who had worked with the F. B. Stearns company before joining Ford, would draw up Ford's ideas on a blackboard, while Henry Ford, sitting in a big rocking chair that had belonged to his mother, would watch and comment. Then the ideas were translated into metal and tested. Much use was made of vanadium steel and special heat treatments of the metal, which gave the new design lightness combined with durability. Transverse springs fore and aft, combined with three-point suspension of the power unit, gave the car a unique ability to cross uneven ground without undue chassis distortion, while a pedal-operated epicyclic transmission developed from that of the Model N gave clash-free gear-changing (a notable boon in those pre-synchromesh days) though it only possessed two forward speeds. This wasn't such a disadvantage as it might have seemed, for the Model T had a 2892 cc engine, which, while its power output was restricted by narrow gas passages, had ample low-speed torque.

When news of the Model T was released to Ford dealers – especially its price of $850 – some of them informed the factory that they had hidden the advance catalogues of the car as its low cost and improved specification would render all the old model Fords still in stock quite unsaleable.

'High priced quality in a low priced car!' shrieked the advertisement which announced Model T to the public on 3 October, 1908, adding: 'We make no apology for the price – any car now selling up to several hundred dollars more could, if built from Ford design, in the Ford factory, by Ford methods, and in Ford quantities, be sold for the Ford price if the makers were satisfied with the Ford profit per car'.

In fact, by the standards of the Model N, the Model T got away to a slow start, only 309 were built in the first three months of production, while Model N output had been running at an average of 70 to 80 cars *a day* during the summer of 1908, reaching a peak of 101 a day as the final orders were met.

By the summer of 1909 output was nudging 2000 cars a month, and the Ford company was claiming 'the largest shipment of motor cars in one consignment in the history of the trade . . . a train of 41 cars, loaded with three motor cars, 123 motor cars in all . . .'. Already, however, it was becoming uneconomic to ship built-up motor cars over long distances, and Ford began to set up branch assembly plants, to which components were shipped in knocked-down form; by 1912 they owned sites in Kansas City, St Louis, Long Island City, Los Angeles, San Francisco, Portland and Seattle, while the first overseas assembly plant had just been established in a former railway carriage works on Britain's first industrial estate, at Trafford Park, Manchester. The plant produced 1485 cars in 1911 and 3081 in 1912, which put it in the front rank of British car manufacturers in terms of volume.

It was just a drop in the ocean against Ford's total output that year in its Detroit factory of 82,400 Model Ts . . .

An important factor in the growth of the Ford Motor Company had been their removal, in the New Year of 1910, to a magnificent new factory at Highland Park, to the northwest of Detroit. Four stories high, 865 feet long and 75 feet wide, this 'Crystal Palace' boasted 50,000 sq ft of glass, and was the largest building under one roof in the state of Michigan. The 60-acre site on which it stood was soon filled with subsidiary buildings. The old Picquette Avenue plant, of which Ford remarked proudly 'As good as, perhaps a little better than, any automobile factory in the country', was sold to Studebaker.

Ford was only following a long American tradition in insisting upon complete and absolute standardisation of components; Samuel Colt, for instance, had used interchangeable parts in his gun factory half-a-century earlier. But at Highland Park, Ford was moving towards a new concept of mass production. It didn't come all at once; there were brilliant individual aspects like the machine which dipped wheels six at a time into vats of paint, spun them round to throw off the surplus and put them out to dry, turning out 2000 wheels a day; or the radiator assembling machine which assembled 50 tubes and plates into a complete matrix in one operation. Then there was the drilling machine

Below: a 1908 Lanchester 20 hp landaulette. Although Lanchesters were way ahead of the rest of the industry in some respects, *ie*, live axles, worm drive and foot accelerators by 1895, models up to 1909 still had lever steering. This vehicle had a disc brake, which operated on the transmission
(National Motor Museum, England)

which bored 45 holes at four different angles in the cylinder block in one operation; most significant was the sub-division of magneto flywheel manufacture into 29 operations performed by 29 men seated along a moving belt, a step which cut the time taken to assemble a magneto progressively from 20 to 13 minutes, then to 7 minutes and finally to 5 minutes.

A similar process was soon adopted for the assembly of the engine, and in the summer of 1913 experiments began in hauling a line of chassis on a rope, six men following each chassis as it was dragged past piles of parts brought to the line in little trucks. An overhead chain hoist dropped the engine into each chassis at the appropriate point. This improvised experiment cut the time taken to assemble each chassis from $12\frac{1}{2}$ hours to 5 hours 50 minutes. Moving production lines were soon installed on a permanent basis, and work further subdivided, so that by the beginning of 1914 it only took 1 hour 33 minutes to assemble each Ford chassis.

Such moves gave spectacular impetus to Ford output; in 1913, 199,100 chassis were produced at Highland Park, while in 1914 the figure rose to 240,700. In 1915, which saw the production of the millionth Model T, 372,250

Fords were manufactured, an achievement which was eclipsed in 1916, which saw 586,202 Ts leave Highland Park, while the following year witnessed the building of 834,662 Ford cars.

It was a total which more than fulfilled the apparently rash statement made a few years previously by Ford's rival, Billy Durant, that one day the American public would buy 500,000 cars every year. Durant, who had tried – and failed – to buy out Ford, had united the Buick, Cadillac and Oldsmobile marques in an organisation which he called General Motors, and for which he had raised capital of $12,500,000. It was, apparently, a winning line-up, especially as Cadillac was headed by Henry M. Leland, the 'Master of Precision', who worked to limits of 100/oooth of an inch, and who had won the British Dewar Trophy in 1908 when three cars had been dismantled, their parts jumbled, and reassembled in the most convincing demonstration of standardisation that had yet been given. However, to its four profitable lines – Buick, Cadillac, Oakland and Oldsmobile – General Motors now added unremunerative dross like the Ewing, Elmore, Cartercar and Rainier, which dragged the group down until, in 1910, the bankers were forced to take over and oust Durant. Under its new president, Charles W. Nash, appointed in 1912, and its works manager, Walter P. Chrysler, General Motors made a spectacular recovery – without the dross.

Durant made a reappearance on the scene as the backer of the new Chevrolet company, which he changed in character from a producer of quality cars to a builder of medium-priced vehicles, made $6,000,000 in six years and regained control of General Motors.

Right: a 1911 Cadillac Model 30, from the stable of Henry M. Leland – 'Master of Precision'. The Model 30 had a four-cylinder engine of 4.7 litres, a three-speed transmission and a double-drop frame which allowed it to sit lower than most touring cars of the period (Hillcrest Motor Co, Beverley Hills, California)

Above, left and below left : one of the last Lion-Peugeots; by 1913 the two Peugeot companies had recombined and were housed under one roof. The C3, of which this is a fine example, was equipped with a V4 engine, as had been tried in some previous models, complete with high-pressure lubrication; the rear wheels were fitted with pedal-operated brakes as well as the two outside handbrake levers shown (Peugeot collection, France)

Morgan were responsible for bringing sporting motoring to those who could not afford large cars, their machines being light enough to be motor-cycle engined. This is a 1927 Morgan Aero, which features a JAP vee-twin power unit (National Motor Museum, England)

was adopted. The bottom tubes of the chassis also served as exhaust pipes, thus keeping the number of parts to a minimum.

Its excellent power-to-weight ratio gave the Morgan a particularly sporting performance, a fact which was not lost on H. F. S. Morgan, who began to enter competitions; he found an enthusiastic, if somewhat unorthodox, 'public relations officer' in his clerical father, Prebendary H. G. Morgan of Stoke Lacy, Worcestershire, who wrote enthusiastically to the press about his son's achievements. He even turned up, clad in top hat with side strings, frock coat and dog-collar, to watch H.F.S. cover sixty miles in the hour at Brooklands in 1912 at the wheel of a special single-seater Morgan. Although various makes of V-twin power unit – MAG, Green-Precision, Blumfield – were used, it was the JAP power unit which became identified with the Morgan.

In the 1913 French Cyclecar Grand Prix, a Morgan came first, and was immediately reclassified as a motor cycle and sidecar by the French authorities for having had the temerity to beat Gallic cyclecars like the Bédélia and the Violet-Bogey; it retained the moral victory.

The Bédélia, produced by two extroverts named Bourbeau and Devaux, was a tandem-seated device which also had its origins in components retrieved after a motor-cycle accident. However, its crude centre-pivot steering, controlled by steel wires wrapped round the tubular column, and belt drive (with ratio changing controlled by the front-seat passenger on racing versions) were

Right: from 1910 to 1950, Morgan three-wheelers were very little changed, having a tubular chassis with sliding-pillar front suspension and quarter-elliptic springs at the rear; engines, however, were another matter, various makes of vee-twin being fitted. The prototype used a Peugeot 7 hp power unit, but the cars which went into production had all kinds of engine, such as JAP and Blumfield

137

His new car used an 1100cc single-cylinder engine (built by Swift) and cost £150; it was not a success, and was soon dropped. Thereafter, the smallest model in Austin's pre-war lineup was an 1145cc 10hp, uprated in 1913 to 1452cc. In that year, incidentally, Austin increased his factory area to nine acres, an addition of 25 per cent, and modernised the production machinery to meet the demand for his products (although the area was marginally reduced again early in 1914 when suffragettes burned down the employees' library).

Others were more faithful to the small-car concept, partly because it brought a new type of customer onto the market: the woman driver. It is often claimed that it was the introduction of the self-starter by Cadillac which really attracted the lady motorist, but in fact the electric starter was a necessary evil which had to be developed once the old trembler-coil ignition system had been ousted by high-tension-magneto or battery-and-coil installations for, while a car in good tune would start on the tremblers once its cylinders had been primed, the more up-to-date ignitions lacked this useful facility.

The advent of lady drivers was not altogether welcomed by a generation of males somewhat apprehensive of the outcome of the emancipation movement. 'Several prominent gentlemen have been assuring us lately that our comrades of the other sex are something of a terror on the roads. If memory serves rightly, most of these gentlemen are somewhat advanced in years. Possibly, when a man has turned the corner of, say, fifty, he objects to piling his new £500 car up the bank in order that a lady piloting her 8hp two-seater may wobble past', commented W. H. Berry in April 1914. 'But, come, sirs! What do we do when any other road obstruction causes delay to our imperial progress? Why, slow down and, if necessary, stop until the danger is past . . . We cannot claim that all women are unsuited to be drivers, forsooth, because some few are inclined to be wobbly on the road. For weal or woe we must make up our minds that the lady driver will be seen on the roads in increasing number . . . Manufacturers are catering specially for the lady driver. They are building cars for her particular benefit, and she is seizing advantage of the opportunity in order to do her shopping and to take out her friends and to run down to town and to the links. What difficulty does the little Swift, or the Humberette, or the Singer, offer a lady driver? Is there any reason why a woman should not handle a Rover, or a Darracq? Assuredly not. Very well then!'

Berry's choice of typical light cars is interesting for, while the Swift and the Humberette were unashamedly cyclecars, albeit of the better-designed sort, the Singer was one of the nicest of all the 'big cars in miniature' to appear in the years immediately preceding World War I. With a four-cylinder engine of 1097cc, the Singer Ten sold for £185 and lasted in basically the same form until 1923. It was a brisk performer, despite having its three-speed gearbox in unit with its rear axle, and it was with a highly tuned version of this model that Lionel Martin, progenitor of the Aston Martin, was to gain experience of rapid light cars.

However, the Singer was only one of several attractive small four-cylinder cars of around 1–1·5 litres capacity to make their début at this period; Calcott and Calthorpe were honoured names, whose origins went back to bicycling days, while Swift added a Ten to their range in 1913 (although it was not nearly as popular as their cyclecar). In Oxford, a successful cycle and motor agent called William Morris was just beginning to market a diminutive model, mostly assembled from proprietory parts. It had a handsome 'bullnosed' brass radiator, a feature shared with the little AC from Thames Ditton, Surrey, which was built as a handsome sporting model as well as in standard two-seater form.

One of the smallest four-cylinder cars to be produced was the little Bébé Peugeot, designed by Ettoré Bugatti, who had not long set up in business as a maker of very expensive, but inordinately rapid, small cars of 1327cc; his Bébé, a design which he had sold to Peugeot, had a monobloc four-cylinder engine of only 855cc and a curious transmission in which the ratios were provided by concentric propeller-shafts terminating in pinions of differing diameters. Normally, the Bébé was endowed with two-seater bodywork rather

Facing page: by 1913, Argyll of Glasgow was the fifth-largest manufacturer in the British Isles, turning out quite a large range of cars. This is a 1913 15/30hp
(National Motor Museum, England)

Left: this elaborately equipped 1914 Turner was originally purchased by a military officer, who was killed shortly afterwards. The car was then stored for sixty years before being found, in original condition
(Cheddar Motor Museum, England)

Below: this 1913 Vauxhall Prince Henry is a 4-litre development of the 3-litre car designed by Laurence Pomeroy Snr for the 1910 Prince Henry Trials. With a four-cylinder, 75 bhp engine it originally sold for £615. It has a top speed of 75–80 mph. Worthy of note are the distinctive bulbous and fluted radiator cowl and the intricate horn
(National Motor Museum, England)

1470 yards in an hour at Brooklands driving a 25 hp Talbot, basically a production touring model, endowed with wind-cheating single-seater body. The fact that, without excessive modification, a car which could be bought for only £515 could put 100 miles into an hour caused a sensation among the motoring public, especially since the speed limit on British roads was only 20 mph (and would remain so until 1930!).

Sunbeam snatched Lambert's record from him with a purpose-built racing car, and 'Pearley', attempting to regain his honours before the opening of the 1913 Motor Show at Olympia, crashed, was killed, and was buried in Brompton Cemetery in a coffin streamlined to match the contours of his car, quite a fitting epitaph to the man.

It was the achievements of men like Lambert which built up the motor business in Britain, despite hostile legislation and official apathy, to the status of a major international industry. In 1905, exports had been only £501,802; in the year ending 31 March 1914, Britain's motor industry exported cars worth £4,324,000. A far sterner test of the industry's abilities was imminent ... on 4 August 1914, World War I began, and with it came the first demands for mechanical transport for military purposes. Although the horse was still favoured by the army at this time, the motor vehicle, in various forms was becoming rapidly more efficient.

CHAPTER 8

The Motor Car goes to War

Left: this 1914 Hallford 3-ton lorry was typical of the kind of vehicle which was used for military purposes at the beginning of World War I. It was powered by a 5.3-litre engine, had chain drive and ran on solid tyres. Later vehicles became more specialised to suit the appalling conditions in which they were often expected to work
(National Motor Museum, England)

Military vehicles had first appeared – except for steam-traction engines – during the Boer War, when a couple of MMC tricycles and a Locomobile steam car had been tentatively used by officers in the British Army, but they had proved of limited utility. The War Office obviously had some idea of the potential of self-propelled vehicles, for they held trials for lorries as early as 1901, and there had been a number of experiments with motorised troop transport on manoeuvres, notably a London–Hastings run organised by the Automobile Association in conjunction with the Guards.

However, the military hierarchy was still enamoured of the horse and, when war broke out in 1914, the Army was woefully short of fighting vehicles. A subsidy scheme had been in operation for some years, under which lorry owners whose vehicles conformed with certain specifications received payments from the War Office on condition that their vehicles were made instantly available for military use on the outbreak of war. The Army obviously had need of them, for its own motorised strength in August 1914 only amounted to some eighty vehicles. Subsidy lorries brought the strength of the British Expeditionary Force's motorised units up to 1200 vehicles. To supplement this inadequate force, the authorities commandeered some 1300 London buses which were shipped over to France for troop transport. Eventually, when time permitted, they were repainted in olive drab, but at first they ploughed their stolid way across the Flanders fields flaunting the bright red livery and boldly lettered advertisements that they had worn on the streets of London.

London taxis, too, were commandeered for service in France, but it was the French who made the first decisive use of internal combustion for military purposes when the military commander of Paris, General Gallieni, commandeered the city's taxis to rush French reinforcements to help stem Von Kluck's advance on the city. It was a decisive move in the Allied victory in the Battle of the Marne, and one of the Renault taxis was preserved for posterity in Les Invalides. Incidentally, the cab-drivers not only received the full cab fare shown on their meters, but also a 27 per cent tip!

Some of the first British vehicles to reach France were quickly involved in the fighting. One three-ton Leyland truck, still bearing the name of 'John Jackson & Son of Bolton & Manchester' on its headboard, was captured by the Germans and later recaptured in damaged condition by Lancashire troops.

Some of the first buses taken over for military use were stripped of their bodywork by the Royal Naval Flying Corps and fitted with boiler-plate armouring. Noted the *War Illustrated*: 'There are a number of British armoured cars at the front, and their services are invaluable for obliterating small parties of German cavalry. The horsemen stand no chance against these swiftly moving and well protected engines of war, unless they vault hedges and ditches and take to the woods, where, naturally, the motor car cannot follow. In the matter of putting an end to the sneaking services of German spies, they are also useful'.

be the standard military issue for staff cars. Roughly, in descending order of rank, the list ran: Rolls-Royce (for the *very* top brass), Vauxhall, Daimler, Sunbeam, Wolseley, Austin and Singer. So strictly was this adhered to that when Sunbeam's output of aero-engines became so great that the company couldn't continue building cars, Rover were contracted to build Sunbeams under licence, even though the Rover car was fully the equal of the Sunbeam for quality.

The Royal Flying Corps (which became the Royal Air Force on 1 April 1918) was an individualistic sort of a service, so it exercised its own choice of motor vehicles, most of its heavy trucks being Leylands, most of its staff cars and tenders Crossleys. So closely did the air service and its transport become linked that the terms 'RAF Leyland' and 'RFC Crossley' were often used as model names.

Individualistic, too, seems to be the only word to describe the attitude of a large part of the French Army to motor transport. Although there was, of course, much standardisation, there were also eccentricities which could not have happened elsewhere. Ambulances were a fruitful medium for self-

Right: artillery batteries are taken to the front at Verdun by 'heavy' lorries of the period; the wheels and tyres on the trucks are all paired to withstand more load, to increase reliability and to reduce the risk of total tyre failure due to gunfire

expression: one conversion consisted of a tandem-seated Bédélia cyclecar (which was driven from the back seat) with a stretcher mounted over the front seat, engine and petrol tank, the last of which was apt to leak on to the hot cylinders and set off a merry blaze. One can imagine the hapless *poilu* pleading to be left to die in peace where he was rather than be rushed off to the field hospital on such a crazy device. An even more casual casualty wagon had appeared in the early stages of the war, however; fitted on the back of a 12/15 hp Mors chassis was a sort of three-storey dishrack, in which the injured were stacked in tiers, completely exposed to the open air. 'Science is required in carrying wounded, a lack of which would often have fatal results', added a cryptic caption. 'Our allies' simple but ingenious method of quickly conveying wounded soldiers from one place to another has proved invaluable in practice.'

A more sensible French conception was the conversion of motor buses into mobile operating theatres.

Where the English used motor cycles for carrying despatches, the French used Bébé Peugeot cars; but where there was a need for rapid communications, Gallic ingenuity received free rein. When war broke out, the Mercédès company, which had just gained a one-two-three victory in the French Grand Prix, was celebrating its win by displaying one of the team cars (under false colours, as they had repainted it with the winning number!) in their showroom

Left: a Cadillac model 55 of 1917; this had a 5.1-litre, V8 engine, producing over 70 bhp and it was in this year that the company introduced detachable cylinder heads for the engine, first produced in 1915
(Skokloster Museum, Sweden)

Right : a Scania-Vabis ambulance of 1914, based on the combine's 20 bhp model; the four-cylinder engine was made with a one-piece cylinder block, as opposed to the two-piece version of the 60 hp model of the same period (Saab-Scania collection)

Below : another De Dion V8 chassis of 1914, in this case specially modified and put to use as an ambulance; despite the obviously cold weather, this particular example seems to have overheated

on the Champs-Elysées. Noted *The Autocar*: 'One of the high officials of the French motor transport service, requiring a car with which he could reel off three or four hundred miles between breakfast and dinner, secured possession of it, to find that connecting rods were broken and the bearings had gone. Put into good mechanical condition, fitted with a windscreen and mudguards, the enemy car rendered valuable service, frequently covering the three hundred miles separating Lyon from Paris after morning business had been attended to, and making another run of about a hundred miles to Châlons, or another point behind the lines. This experience showed that a racing car can be used very successfully for long distance travel, for the officer who had charge of the Mercédès states that his petrol consumption was eighteen miles to the gallon, that tyre trouble was practically nil, and that the car was so easy to handle that after three hundred miles he was not too fatigued to work'.

Another ex-racing car used for high-speed dashes was the Renault which had won the 1906 French Grand Prix; this car was appropriated by the celebrated Escadrille Cigogne ('Stork Squadron') of the French Air Services, who thought that it would be 'a suitable machine for wild dashes from the front to the base, from camp to Paris or from point to point of the line'. Despite its 10 mpg petrol consumption, and tyres which refused to last for more than 500 miles, the Renault was used with success by the leading French air aces –

Guynemer, Fonck, Nungesser and Navarre.

Perhaps the most hilarious conversion was that carried out by the Italians on the 115 hp Itala which Henri Fournier had driven in the 1908 Grand Prix at Dieppe; this was converted into an ambulance to make a nightly climb up a mountainside in search of wounded on the border between Austria and Italy. But the machine was so unsuitable for the task, and ran so badly that the secret police became suspicious of its activities, and arrested the driver and passenger, keeping them under observation for twelve hours until their innocence could be proved . . .

Keeping all these diverse Allied vehicles supplied with petrol was an immense task in itself, and sterling work was carried out by the petrol companies, both in shipping crude oil from the oilfields, despite the constant threat of U-Boat attack, and in refining it and getting it to the Front. Shell, indeed, built a refinery, shipped it across the Channel one weekend, and had it working within 36 hours. Even the humble two-gallon petrol tin played its part: a special factory was set up for the manufacture of this indispensible item, which, when drained of spirit, was used for countless purposes in the trenches – even as building blocks for shelters and, after being beaten flat, as flooring for the trench.

The Germans, who had entered the war somewhat better equipped with military motors than the Allies – as early as 1900 the Kaiser had offered a prize equivalent to £4000 for the 'best automobile war carriage which will combine all the requisites for service in the field' – suffered badly from the British naval blockade. As their supplies of rubber dwindled, the Germans were forced to resort to all kinds of substitute spring metal tyres, which proved a great hindrance to their mobility. Their choice of staff cars fully reflected their highly class-structured society, ranging down from Field Marshal Von Hindenburg's 21-litre Benz tourer (which still exists in England . . .) to the sub-utility 10 hp Phanomobil, which had its single-cylinder engine mounted above the front wheel. This eccentric tricycle was more often seen in the guise of a delivery van. Komnick, Opel and Stoewer were other makes favoured by the Kaiser's armies.

The unparalleled use of mechanical traction during World War I was to prove of major significance in the future growth of the motor industry. Thousands of men, whose peacetime experience of motor vehicles was no more than a rare ride on an omnibus – if that – had been trained as drivers and mechanics, and tasted the rare mobility that only the rich motor owner had known pre-war. Having tested, and fought for, that sense of freedom they were unlikely now to look back.

Right: an Ehrhardt armoured car, built for the German forces and known as a street wagon

Right and below: a strange German vehicle, the Phanomobile 6/12ps; this particular example, with a transverse, air-cooled, four-cylinder engine mounted over and chain-driving the tiller-steered front wheel, was manufactured in 1922, but earlier examples of the model had been used by the German army as ambulances during World War I. Primary drive was by friction to a two-speed epicyclic gearbox, while, as one photograph shows, cooling was aided by twin fans
(National Motor Museum, England)

be repaid in the spring of 1921, a figure which, taken with outstanding tax bills and employee bonuses, added up to over $50,000,000 – or $30,000,000 more than the company's cash reserves). A crash programme of waste elimination was carried out, and the company stopped buying raw materials, and stockpiled cars using the materials on hand, thus saving costs.

Throughout November and December 1921, the leading motor manufacturing companies began to close down their factories 'for stocktaking', and thousands of men were laid off. On Christmas Eve, Ford closed down 'for inventory' too. Within three months, the number of men employed in the motor industry in Detroit had fallen from 176,000 to 24,000.

Managers laid a machine-shop floor in the Ford factory, and when that was done, acted as watchmen, patrolling the empty buildings on bicycles and roller skates. Office staff were dismissed in their hundreds, and all the spare office and catering equipment was sold, raising an estimated $7,000,000. But these dark days were the nadir of the depression; in January there were signs that car sales were picking up again in New York, and some manufacturers began production again. The Ford plant remained shut, however, with demand met by dealers' stocks, built-up cars which Ford had stockpiled and vehicles assembled from spare parts at the Ford branch factories. At the end of January, Highland Park opened up again, and Ford began shipping cars out to dealers, to be paid for on delivery. Thus, instead of having to borrow the money needed to pay off his $50,000,000 debts, Ford compelled his dealers to borrow to pay for the cars. Most of them found little difficulty in disposing of the extra vehicles as sales continued to recover through the spring of 1921. Once again, Henry Ford had proved his ability to survive in adverse conditions.

The slump was slower in reaching Britain: the postwar boom began to collapse at the end of 1920, and it was not until the spring of 1921 that the full effects were felt. William Morris, now entering the mass-production market with his Morris-Cowley, saw sales plunge from 288 in October 1920 to 68 in January 1921. He reacted by following the Ford lead and slashing prices, knocking £100 off a £525 Cowley four-seater, and reducing other models by figures ranging from £25 to £90. Other makers, notably Bean, had earlier cut prices, but Morris had chosen the right psychological moment, and succeeded where the others had failed. Not only did his sales increase – his profits rose, too.

The collapse of the post-Armistice boom was also to provide Morris with his keenest competitor, although in a somewhat circuitous fashion. The Clyno Manufacturing Company of Wolverhampton were one of the country's most respected makers of motor cycles, whose machines had been widely used during the war (one of their motor-cycle machine-gun outfits can still be seen in London's Imperial War Museum), in which they had developed an ohv four-cylinder power unit originally intended as the motive power for a sidecar combination. However, Frank Smith, the company's Managing Director, was an enthusiast for sporting light cars, and decided to enter the car market after the war with a 10hp ohv four-cylinder model using the motor-cycle engine, which could almost have been the British equivalent of the Brescia Bugatti; three prototypes were built before the company's backers, De La Rue, withdrew their finances and Clyno went into Receivership. Reformed in 1922, Clyno abandoned both motor cycles and sporting light cars and instead moved into the mass-production market, building a 10·8hp model, largely from bought-in components, powered by a side-valve Coventry-Climax engine. Right from the start, Frank Smith followed the Morris star, continually trimming the prices of Clyno models so that they were identical to those of the equivalent Morrises. It was a policy which worked spectacularly well – at first – raising Clyno eventually to third place in the British production league behind Morris and Austin, at which stage they were producing 300 cars a week in a tiny factory in the heart of Wolverhampton, its inadequate floor space augmented by an asbestos roof over the dirt yard outside.

One of the reasons for the popularity of the Clyno was its excellent handling, which was apparent right from the earliest. In April 1923, *The Autocar* took one of the first few hundred Clynos on the road, and was highly impressed . . . 'It is curious how obvious in the running of a new car is the handiwork of the

Below: a 1927 10.8hp Clyno Royal Tourer, with coachwork by Mulliner. By following Morris's price-cutting marketing strategy, Clyno became Britain's third biggest seller, behind Morris themselves and Austin. Alas, Clyno's standards were forced into decline by this policy and the firm survived only until 1929

designer who is also an artistic driver. For example, the family model Clyno handles in such a way which suggests that those who are responsible for it understand very fully the finer points of roadworthiness and have attended to each with exceeding care. As a result, there is, indeed, very little to criticise and much to commend'.

One reason for the good handling of the car was the fact that one of the firm's backers apparently owned a Grand Prix Peugeot, and specified that the Clyno should have steering that was equally light and positive. In this, the Clyno's designer, George Stanley, who had previously worked for the Triumph motorcycle company, was entirely successful: 'It must be admitted that the Clyno steering gear is one of the best . . . the necessity of effort is so small that the car is steered as unconsciously as a bicycle'.

Although the Clyno company built some components (like the gearbox) themselves, the Clyno was still largely an assembled car, albeit a very successful one. One reason for its steadily rising sales graph was probably that it bore an established and respected name with a good war record, which would have overcome the sales resistance felt by an entirely new marque. In this respect,

it is interesting to observe the fate of the Cooper, a handsome light car also introduced in 1922, which used almost exactly the same mechanical mix as the Clyno. This marque lasted one year, and produced perhaps forty cars; Clyno lasted nine years and sold nearly 40,000.

Another factor which sorted, in the public's eye at least, the sheep from the goats as far as light cars were concerned was the burgeoning number of trials.

These trials were not just Sunday afternoon map-reading exercises, either; take the 1921 Scottish Six Days' Trial, which covered 900 miles 'deliberately designed to smash up every frangible part of the machines'. It included such fearsome ascents as Tornapress and Applecross, where the road rose steadily for five miles on end, 'stony cart tracks in regions chiefly inhabited by sheep, eagles and deer . . . they have a knack of topping off a frightful bottom gear grind with two or three C corners on a grade of one in five, with a road width so restricted that a car must be reversed to get round. Or take Inverfarigaig Corkscrew, a 6ft track, paved with dust or mud (according to the weather, and doubling back in itself six times within 800 yards; at each hairpin, the inside wheel must clamber up one in five or six, while the outer wheel races up a comparatively mild pitch of one in eight . . . The trial is run on a basis of 20 mph, plus or minus five minutes per hour. Twenty miles in sixty-five minutes on the Portsmouth Road is, of course, child's play, even for a tiny car, but Scotland has no equivalent for the Portsmouth Road. In the loch districts, a so-called main road swirls along in a precarious serpentine switchback, full of humps, dips, blind angles, and the most poisonous little skew bridges, too narrow for a pair of vehicles and generally quite invisible till the last second. Such a road spells violent acceleration and violent brake work . . . it makes for chassis testing'.

Above: the most famous precursor of the modern baby car was the Austin Seven. The Seven offered seats for four, 45 mph and brakes on all wheels. This is a 1923 'Chummy' with a fold-down hood. Like the Model T, the Seven came in many guises, from racing cars to delivery vans, and it was built under licence throughout the world. It fulfilled admirably the intention of its designer, Sir Herbert Austin, to bring motoring to a vast new market

Such conditions would prove a stiff test for modern small cars, yet of the fifteen light cars taking part in the trial, fourteen finished, ten won gold medals, one a silver and three were awarded bronzes. The car which retired was an 8 hp air-cooled, two-cylinder Rover, which ran off the road into a ditch and broke a spring. 'The other four Rover Eights all won gold medals, losing no time and climbing all the hills', reported *The Autocar*. 'This is simply a stupendous performance . . . They did not smoke, they did not smell hot and oily, and they very rarely gave an audible pink even when they had to pick up on a fierce grade after a terrible hairpin at the top of a long climb. They have scored a great triumph for air cooling, and their success possibly sounds the tocsin for the big sidecar.'

In fact, the car which was to prove the doom of the sidecar outfit as a common means of family transport was probably no more than a doodle on the back of an envelope when those words were written, for it was in 1922 that Sir Herbert Austin announced his new 7 hp baby car, which he had designed on the billiard table at his home to avoid the criticism of colleagues opposed to the project. The Austin Seven was designed to occupy the same ground area as a motor cycle and sidecar, and it *did* look ridiculously small and pramlike to British eyes (although the Continentals were well used to tiny cars); but, like the Model T Ford, it was designed for that section of the market that hitherto could not afford a car. The initial scorn and derision which greeted its announcement turned to admiration when the aviation pioneer E. C. Gordon England decided to prove the new car's mettle. Nearly fifty years later, the author interviewed him about the competition début of the Austin Seven, and his recollections of the events of 1922 were still crystal-clear.

'I'd crashed in the *Daily Mail* gliding contest at Itford, in Sussex, and I was laid up in hospital at Eastbourne for some weeks with my leg in plaster right up to the knee. It was this that started me off, because I was lying in bed recovering and I read all about this new Austin Seven. One thing that became rooted in my mind was: "He'll never sell this thing, because it's being described in the motor press as a toy – and the public won't buy toys, they want cars".

'I went into it very thoroughly, and came to the conclusion that the Austin Seven would make a very good show as a racing car. So I wrote to Sir Herbert Austin, as he was in those days, and said: "I am intrigued by this car, but I

Below: a 1923 Hotchkiss AM Tourer, with coachwork by Melhuish. The AM, built at St Denis, Seine, had a four-cylinder, side-valve engine of 2.4 litres, a four-speed gearbox and four-wheel brakes

don't see how you are going to get it over to the public unless you can hit them squarely between the eyes from the word go – and the only way to do that is to race it. I've taken the trouble to go into the whole position very carefully, and I find that Brooklands has a whole series of 750 cc class records. Not one of them has ever been touched.

'"Therefore, if you do what I suggest, you can go out and get all these records – I'm certain you can set them at over 70 mph – you can go before the public announcing the availability of 'the Austin Seven, which has already taken all these records at Brooklands.'

'"At present, I am in hospital recovering from a damaged leg, but as soon as I'm mobile, may I come up and have a chat with you about the whole idea"?

'I got a very nice letter back, saying that he'd be glad to see me and perhaps I'd let him know when I was fit to travel. In due course, I was released from hospital, and the first thing I did was to go up to Longbridge. "Before I go and see Sir Herbert", I thought, "I'd better find out just what the climate is like here". Well, the climate was what I'd expected – I might almost say hoped! – the whole staff thought the old man was going soft in the head. I had a long chat with the sales manager, a very brusque fellow, who said "The whole thing's nonsense . . . they'll never sell!".

'"Isn't that marvellous", I thought. "This is the chap who's going to put this car on the market!".

'Having got this view, and one or two others quite similar, I marched in to see Sir Herbert Austin. Now he had a secretary called Howitt, who had a most peculiar squeaky voice. "He's in there", he said, nodding towards Austin's door, "but I don't think you'll do anything with him".

'However, I walked in, and Austin was perfectly polite, really . . . for him! He said, very gruffly: "Well, what do you want?".

'Then we had a two-hour battle straight off. He opposed every mortal thing I said – and I told him he didn't know what he was talking about. We really got down to a slogging match, which was inevitable with him – it was his nature – and I said: "Look here, I've been round your organisation, and you haven't got a friend in the place. They don't believe the Austin Seven's got any future at all. The only way you can get round it is by doing what I suggest".

'Towards the end of the two hours, I think I'd beaten him down on every point. He didn't like that very much, so his final gambit was, I think, a lovely one. Pointing at my leg in plaster, he said: "You'd make a bloody fine racing driver!".

'"You damned fool", I replied – we'd got to that stage then – "You couldn't build a racing car by the time that leg's all perfectly sound!".

'"Can't I?", he said. "All right, that's a bet!".

'And that's how we ended the conversation – he muttered something about "he'd bloody well show me". So I went home and carried on with my business, getting fit among other things. One day I received a telegram: "RACING CAR ON TRAIN NO . . . ARRIVING PADDINGTON . . . O'CLOCK. PLEASE MEET AND COLLECT. HERBERT AUSTIN".

'He'd won . . . I still had my leg in plaster. He must have gone at it like a bull at a gate to get the thing done. I went up to collect it, and there it was – shockingly badly interpreted from what I'd asked for, I thought, but the essentials were there. That was all I cared about. I knew I could do the rest. So I took the car straightaway to my little works at Walton-on-Thames, full of joy because I hadn't expected to get it so soon, and we set about making it run.

'In those days, I saw a lot of Sammy Davis. "I'm going for records at Brooklands", I said. "Can I count on you to come and help me?"

'"Of course you can", he said. Then I knew I had *The Autocar* behind me.

'Dear old Lindsay Lloyd, the Clerk of the Course at Brooklands, was himself all over . . . "You can't do anything in *that* car!", he said.

'"Never mind", I replied. "Will you be there, because we want all the tapes down for the mile and half-mile and so on".

'Well, as luck would have it, the little car behaved awfully well, and Lindsay Lloyd reported back that we'd done the half-mile at 75·8 mph, I think it was, and the mile at 72 mph. We'd lost some speed because we'd gone round on to

Below: the Austin Seven was built with many identities in many countries. This is a Dixi 3/15 hp, two-seater roadster, built in Germany. In 1928, the Dixi works were absorbed by BMW and the model continued as the BMW-Dixi

the banking. Anyway, it was very good.

'I was able to telegraph back to Sir Herbert Austin that we had set up the records. And that was the beginning of the Austin Seven!'.

That, too, was the end of the cyclecar, which had reared its unlovely head again in the post-Armistice boom, due partly to the tremendous amount of Government surplus material which was dumped on the market at knockdown prices. Timber and ply featured large in the make-up of many of the nastier cyclecars – I once saw the remnants of a Gibbons, manufactured in suburban Essex by two incurable optimists named Gibbons and Moore: it resembled nothing more than a tea-chest mounted, somewhat haphazardly, on four old

Above and far right: this fine example of the rare 1923 Humber Chummy was restored by Humber apprentices. It is powered by a four-cylinder 8 hp engine
(Coventry Motor Museum, England)

Below and right: what must have been one of the most successful 'Unusual' cars ever built, the Leyland Motors-manufactured Trojan. This 1924 car featured a four-cylinder, two-stroke engine mounted under the floor. Although the power output from its 1½ litres was a miniscule 10 bhp, its pulling up steep hills at low speed was quite remarkable. Solid tyres were available on these cars right up until 1929
(National Motor Museum, England)

pram wheels, with a motor bike engine bolted on the offside. In 1921 this unlovely machine sold for £115 – which must have represented a profit of around 900 per cent on the material costs – and a 'set of fittings' (presumably luxuries like hood, windscreen and lights) was another £18.

The advent of the Austin Seven, a proper four-cylinder, four-seater car for £165 fully equipped, consigned such aberrations to the everlasting bonfire they so richly deserved; it also proved the salvation of the Austin company, whose other post-war products could be summed up as 'worthy'; well engineered, they were ponderous machines which had lost all the excitement of the pre-1914 Austins, which rejoiced in model names like 'Vitesse' and 'Defiance'. Herbert Austin's post-war policy had initially been to produce a 20 hp model which adapted American design philosophies to British taste, and, insofar as the Austin Twenty was really rather a dull machine, he succeeded admirably; its younger sister, the Austin Heavy Twelve, which followed soon after as a sop to the horsepower tax, was another well engineered car which was totally lacking in 'sparkle', and was said to be much favoured by maiden aunts (as a digression, uncles seemed to go for Morris Oxfords, but one's father tended to favour the Clyno; thus early did popular cars acquire a 'market image').

More attractive light cars appeared in 1922: there was the pretty little 8/18 Talbot, designed by Louis Coatalen and sold in France with a different radiator as the Darracq by another component of the Sunbeam-Talbot-Darracq combine in one of the earliest successful examples of corporate badge engineering; there was the 8/18 Humber, with its close-coupled 'chummy' bodywork; there was the attractive Gwynne Eight, unique among British cars in being taken originally from a Spanish design, the Madrid-built Victoria, whose progenitor, Arturo Elizalde, was normally associated with the production of large, luxurious, sporting cars; and there was the Trojan . . .

The Trojan was designed by Leslie Hounsfield, who had made his name as a designer of steam-propelled military transport at the time of the Boer War, which may explain some of the more curious features of the car's eccentric make-up. Hounsfield had built a prototype of his 'people's car' as early as 1910, but it wasn't until he had attracted Leyland Motors, who had prospered greatly

Left and below: André Citroën brought to the slightly anachronistic French motor industry at least a breath of the methods that car manufacturers throughout the world had long regarded as *de rigeur*. While his countrymen clung to archaic methods of production, Citroën, in 1919, put his version of mass production into practice. This is one of his second generation of cars, the 1925 5cv tourer. The famous double chevron Citroën badge commemorates André Citroën's former trade as a gear cutter

French mass-producers, however, built solid cars of almost indestructible reliability; and of those mass-producers the most spectacular was André Citroën, who had worked for Mors before the war, and had emerged in 1919 as the first European manufacturer truly to assimilate the Ford system of mass-production of a single model. In his new factory on the Quai de Javel, Citroën proposed to build one hundred cars a day, which would be sold, fully equipped, at a moderate price . . . and received 30,000 orders before production began. Citroën's first car was the 10cv Type A four-cylinder tourer.

He was even inspired to announce grandiose plans for a factory in America, but this scheme was soon abandoned. However, Citroën did establish an assembly plant in England as well as subsidiaries in other European countries. The English works, at Brook Green, Hammersmith, was opened in 1923, by which time Citroën had announced the Type B, an improved version of the Type A, and the little 5cv which, since it was normally seen in bright yellow paintwork, was punningly known as the 'Citroën pressée', which phonetically could be rendered either as 'Citroën in a hurry' or 'lemon squash!'.

For the English market, Citroën imported the Type B in chassis form, coachwork, in the British idiom, being fitted by Short Brothers of Rochester, Kent, another firm of aircraft builders who had turned to car-body manufacture in the post-war slump. The little 5cv was imported complete from Paris. Then, in 1925, Citroën pioneered the all-steel body built under the American

A beautiful exa
37.2hp model;
specially comm
Alwar in 1929
and it has cabr
French coachb
intended prima
spotlights mou
were intended
having extenda
focussed on the
in front of the
the cockpit and
(Stratford Mot

Below and right: this imposing vehicle is a Standard 13.9 hp all-weather tourer of 1926, built by the Standard Motor Company of Coventry, which was founded by R. W. Maudslay in 1903. The 13.9 hp, introduced in 1924, used an overhead-valve engine and worm final drive; it was the company's most successful offering of the period. The radiator mascot, which was adopted in 1923, is the standard of the ninth Roman Legion

CHAPTER 10

The Death of the Cyclecar

If proof was needed that the motor vehicle was an essential part of everyday life, then it came in May 1926, when the Trades Union Council called upon Union members throughout Britain to support the miners, whose industry had been badly hit by lower-priced German and Polish coal, as well as by newer sources of energy – oil and electricity. At midnight on Monday 3 May, in defiance of emergency regulations which made it an offence to 'prevent the proper use or working of any . . . railway, canal, bridge, road, tramway, vehicle . . .', railwaymen and transport workers joined the ranks of the strikers.

For a few hours, the nation ground to a halt, and then volunteers came in to keep the roads and railways moving; the 'unprecedented interference with routine' lasted until 15 May (although the miners stayed out until August). During that period, those who could drive took over trucks and buses – buses were festooned with barbed wire and carried a policeman to keep the strikers at bay, although the only serious incident occurred when strikers overturned a Tilling-Stevens petrol-electric of Thomas Tilling's fleet at the Elephant and Castle. There were, indeed, some curious sights; well-known racing drivers at the controls of lorries and buses, a $10\frac{1}{2}$-litre Fiat racing car delivering copies of the Government newspaper, *The British Gazette* . . .

The private car came into its own, carrying people to and from work, and London had a foretaste of things to come, with traffic jams and parking problems; Hyde Park was closed off, and became a distribution centre for milk and fish, while Regent's Park was used as a bus depot at night. Vans and trucks were converted into impromptu buses, too, carrying commuters in from the suburbs in extreme discomfort for 3d to 6d. There was, it seems, no problem in getting hold of petrol, and the brand-new miracle of wireless kept the nation informed of the progress of the strike.

It would be foolish to assume that things went on as normal, but thanks to motor vehicles, abnormality was kept to a minimum. And when it was all over, *The Autocar* commented: 'During the troublous times through which we have all passed one outstanding point emerges, and this is the paramount importance of road transport to the whole community. In the days before the motor vehicle had become a part of our national life the discontinuance of work on so gigantic a scale as that which took place when the general strike was declared would almost certainly have resulted in a paralysis of activity utterly disastrous to every branch and section of the people. In our opinion, the escape of the country with wounds which, deep though they may be, will heal in time, is attributable to the fact that road transport of essential commodities was available to save the nation from irreparable disaster'.

Certainly, the Strike started the habit of commuting by car, and only a few days after one enthusiastic motorist was writing to the Minister of Transport suggesting that 'motorists who drive into London daily to business should be given special facilities in the parking places nearest their offices, and by being allowed a four hours stay instead of the two hours at present available'.

quite "unhealthy" after the unwanted incident on what was to all events her "maiden voyage".

'I can honestly assure you that during my many years of motoring, I have never witnessed such a mean action performed upon a fellow motorist by another supposed loyal member of our colossal motoring fraternity. It completely filled me with utter disgust, and it is evidently some small sample of treatment that one may possibly expect to receive from some of the so-called "Ladies" encountered on the road'.

As a postscript, one may add that at this period – and, indeed, right up to 1930, there was no compulsion on motorists to take out insurance against accidents. Nor was there any form of driving test, two factors which add extra point to this account of a mid 1920s escapade which reads like the scenario of a Mack Sennett comedy: 'On coming to the crossing from the direction of Rugeley, it was apparently deserted, but, my attention being on the signpost ahead to find the road for London, I unfortunately failed to notice the turning coming out at an angle on my left, from which a number of cars and motor cycles were coming and evidently wishing to go to Warwick.

An Austro-Daimler ADS 19/100hp of 1926, powered by a straight-six overhead-camshaft engine of 3 litres, whose 100bhp can push the car along at a speed of 100mph. This example is believed to be the 1926 Ulster TT machine

Left: the 11.9 hp AC of 1921, with a four-cylinder, side-valve Anzani engine with a three-speed gearbox, mounted on the rear axle; the car relied for its stopping power on a single transmission brake
(National Motor Museum, England)

'Failing to locate the London road from the signpost, I decided to drive up to the policeman on the point to inquire. Shouts on my left caused me to realise that I had brought my car almost broadside on to the traffic emerging on that side.

'Seeing they had all managed to slow sufficiently to clear me, I again started to make for the policeman, when a car seemed to appear from nowhere, coming head on. Seeing a turning on my left I accelerated and swung into it, as my only hope of preventing a nasty collision, my action again throwing those unfortunate people on my left into confusion.

'At this moment, the policeman, who had evidently been taking a little relaxation from his undoubted strenuous job of regulating the traffic, woke up and in a loud voice inquired what game I thought I was playing. I did not stop to tell him, as I had done no damage, and shuddered to think of the names I might be called if I returned among my victims'.

Mind you, the motoring laws in Britain were so antiquated that it would have been difficult, even for the most law-abiding citizen, to have remained within them. George Bernard Shaw, always ready for a good controversy, claimed that between 1909 and 1929 he had covered well over 100,000 miles, and had never completed a car journey without breaking the law . . . at the time, he was addressing the Chief Constables' Conference! Shaw was quite proud of the fact that he had been summoned for speeding: 'I was informed that I had passed through a police control at a speed of twenty-seven miles an hour. There was no question. There was no room for argument. The constable and I were perfectly civil to one another. He was pleased when he got my name, because he knew he would be in the paper next day. And I was pleased, because what came into my head was that it was a mercy he did not catch me half an hour before, when I was driving at fifty!'.

So, motoring was becoming more commonplace. But what were the makes which made it so? Whose cars were the most popular? We can gain some idea, at least, from the various impromptu censuses which enthusiasts compiled for publication in the correspondence columns of the motoring press. On a Sunday afternoon in Sussex in the summer of 1925, a motorist counted the number of cars using the Bognor-Littlehampton road during the space of an hour: 'Morris 29, Austin 15, Rover 15, Singer 13, Ford 11, Standard 8, Bean and Citroën 5, Wolseley 6, Dodge Brothers 4, Talbot 4, Daimler and Clyno 2, AC 4, Overland 4, Essex 4, Sunbeam 4, Buick 3, Napier 3, Hillman 3, Renault 3, Armstrong-Siddeley 4, Fiat 5, Morgan and Chevrolet 2, Crossley and Humber 3, Unic 2 and one each of the following: Studebaker, Swift, Delage, Charron-Laycock, Lancia, Riley, ABC, Cubitt, GWK, Star, Darracq and Jowett'.

On the Continent, obviously, things were a little different. Four years later, an inhabitant of that cosmopolitan and somewhat anti-motorist country, Switzerland, made a similar survey of the cars passing his house in Geneva

Left and below: this imposing vehicle is a 1925
Austro Daimler ADM/BK, powered by an
overhead-camshaft, six-cylinder engine and
designed by the brilliant Ferdinand Porsche
(National Motor Museum, England)

Right : Humber's 14/40 Doctor's Coupé of 1927;
it featured a four-cylinder engine of 2050 cc and
had a top speed of just on 60 mph
(Coventry Motor Museum, England)

Below and below right : the AC Six of 1925
featured a six-cylinder, overhead-camshaft engine
designed by John Weller. In 1991 cc form, the
engine produced a highly respectable 40 bhp, and
it was still in production, albeit in a modified
state, in 1963. By this time, it was producing over
100 bhp
(Peter Hampton)

Above: Peugeot's Type 163 of 1923, which is powered by a 1437 cc, 10 hp, four-cylinder engine. This is the Torpedo version, but the model was also available with de luxe Torpedo or boat-tailed, sporting four-seater bodywork (Peugeot Collection, France)

between 5.50 pm and 6.20 pm one Sunday – and a curiously mixed bag they were: Citroën 43; Fiat 43; Peugeot 22; Renault 21; Chrysler 20; Buick 10; Ford 9; Whippet 7; Talbot, Donnet, De Dion, Nash, 6 each; Delage, Studebaker, 5 each; Ansaldo, Auburn, Erskine, Essex, 4 each; Amilcar, Cadillac, Chenard-Walcker, Pic-Pic, Voisin, 3 each; Martini, Benz, Imperia, Panhard, Packard, Willys-Knight, Wolseley, Victory, Austin, Bugatti, Minerva, Frazer-Nash, Aries, 2 each; Lancia, Sizaire, DeSoto, Opel, Falcon-Knight, Ballot, Berliet, LaSalle, Chevrolet, Maximag, Rally, Mathis, Hudson, 1 each. British cars, our observer added, were almost unknown on the roads of his country, only the odd Morris, Austin or Rolls-Royce serving to remind the Swiss that Britain did indeed have a motor industry.

The sad thing about Britain's apparent indifference to export sales was that the average British-built car was demonstrably equal to the most extreme overseas conditions – a standard 10.8 hp Clyno, with no pump or fan to aid its cooling, was reported to be in everyday use in Aden without any overheating troubles. In 1926, Frank Grey, the former MP for Oxford, challenged the British motor industry to build him a car suitable for making the West-East crossing of Africa; the only response came from Jowett of Bradford. On 16 May 1926, Grey and his companion, Jack Sawyer, left Lagos in two two-seater Jowett 7 hp flat-twin cars. Sixty days and 3800 miles later, they arrived at Massawa, on the Red Sea, after an adventurous trip, during which they had freed a young native girl from slave traders. Jowett, who specialised in coining advertising slogans – typical samples included 'The little engine with the big pull' and 'The seven that passes a seventeen like a seventy' – now added 'The car that put the camel on the dole' to the list.

British cars, too, had made the first motor journey from Cape to Cairo a few months earlier; Major and Mrs Chaplin Court Treatt had started the epic 13,000-mile journey on 24 September 1924, driving a pair of 25 hp Crossleys, which reached their destination on 24 January 1926, having survived the muddiest rainy season on record. In 1927 Mrs Diana Strickland crossed Africa in a Wolverhampton-built 14/40 hp Star named 'The Star of the Desert'.

On other continents, too, British cars blazed the trails: in 1924 Major Forbes-Leith's Wolseley 14 had been the first car to make the journey by road from England to India.

The British did not, however, have a monopoly of long-distance motoring,

Below and bottom: while Citroën are justly famous for their front-wheel-drive cars, they have also produced some notable rear-drive vehicles, the most extreme of which was this half-track conversion by M Kegresse. Many French colonies were in inaccessible West Africa, protected by thousands of miles of desert. It was an expedition of comprehensively equipped Citroën Kegresses which made the first successful crossing of the Sahara, in 1922–3. Similar vehicles went on to make many other pioneering journeys

for Citroëns fitted with the half-track conversion devised by M. Kégresse, formerly in charge of the garages of His Imperial Majesty the Tsar of all the Russias, were renowned for opening roads across Africa, where the French had long been trying to establish closer links with their colonies; French West Africa was separated from Algeria by several thousand miles of desert. The equipment carried by the Citroëns, which made the first successful Sahara crossing in 1922–23 is worthy of note. Wrote André Citroën: 'The body was designed to give the maximum of comfort to the travellers. It had three seats, one of them reserved for a possible guide, boxes of provisions, camp requisites, maps and munitions – for, in the desert, one must think of defence, and the mission carried a rifle per man and three aeroplane machine-guns. Each car carried, rolled up on its side, a tent which could be built up in a few minutes. Two of them, called provision cars, carried from 60 to 120 gallons of

petrol. The others had two tanks of 15 gallons each, making 50 gallons with the front tank. They also had two water tanks, holding four gallons'.

In 1924–25, came the famous *Croisière Noire* (Black Journey) in which eight cars were despatched from Algeria, to cross Africa, splitting into four groups which would reach the coast at Mombasa, Dar-es-Salaam, Mozambique and Cape Town, finally to rendezvous again on the island of Madagascar, having carried out 'a feat of transport unsurpassed in the history of the motor car'.

Then, in 1931, Georges Haardt, organiser of these two journeys, achieved the crossing of Asia from Turkestan to Peking at the head of an expedition of Citroën *auto-chenilles* christened *La Croisiere Jaune* (Yellow Journey), only to die from pneumonia in Hong Kong while planning the return trip.

Turning from the well planned to the near-farcical; in 1926 three Chinese men made the overland trip from Shanghai in a beaten-up Trojan, arriving in London to tumultuous apathy (although, along with Parry Thomas, who had just taken the Land Speed Record at 171.09 mph in his 27-litre *Babs*, they were honoured at a supper and concert party organised by Leyland Motors whose engine was used in Thomas's car).

Facing page : the last Mercedes-Benz car to be built at Mannheim and the last one designed by Dr Porsche – the Nürburg 460 of 1928. Power was from a straight-eight, overhead-camshaft engine of 4.6 litres and the car featured the classic Mercedes U-section frame, rigid axles and semi-elliptic springs

Below : by the time this Model T sedan was built, in 1926, sales of Ford's classic had begun a rapid decline from a peak of over two million in the 1923 fiscal year. While Henry Ford clung steadfastly to his devotion to the T, rivals reaped the benefits. Ford eventually admitted defeat in 1927 and the T was replaced

Then there was Michael Terry who, with £8 2s 3d in his pocket, set out in February 1923 at the wheel of a rickety Ford, accompanied by one Richard Yockney, to make the first-ever crossing of the desolate 'Never Never Land' of Northern Australia, covering 800 miles of trackless desert where, on occasion, the car could only cover ten yards at a time before becoming bogged down, and where four miles could represent a day's journey. And when they reached their destination in October (after running out of both petrol and water in the desert and almost dying before a search party found them), the explorers felt so uncomfortable in the soft beds of the hotel that they rolled themselves in blankets and slept on the bare boards of the verandah!

However, although the Model T Ford was still capable of conquering the desert, during the mid 1920s, its star, which had seemed permanently in the ascendant, began to wane with alarming rapidity as old age caught up with the 'Universal Car'. Sales, which had reached a peak of 2,055,309 during the company's fiscal year (August to July) of 1923, fell off, slowly at first, then with increasing rapidity as Ford's rivals introduced more attractive models that were not just a 1908 design gently warmed over like the Model T. Henry

Ford, who had envisaged the car going on for ever, was nonplussed as customers turned to the more stylish Overland, Essex, Chevrolet and Dodge models. As speculation grew that the T was approaching the end of production, with some 14 million of the type already built, Ford remained adamant, denying all rumours. 'We have no intention of introducing a "six"', he stated in December 1926. 'The Ford car is a tried and proved car that requires no tinkering. It has met all the conditions of transportation the world over . . . Changes in style from time to time are merely evolution . . . We do not intend to make a "six", an "eight" or anything else outside of our regular products. It is true that we have experiments with such cars, as we have experiments with many things. They keep our engineers busy – prevent them from tinkering too much with the Ford car.'

Ford had, indeed, planned a successor to the Model T, the unorthodox eight-cylinder X-Car, so-called because its cylinders were laid out in the form of two St Andrew's Crosses in tandem, but the engine proved too heavy, and the sparking plugs on the lower cylinders so susceptible to water and mud that the design was shelved in 1926, after six years of experimentation.

Rumours that the Model T was to be discontinued after nineteen years' production began to spread. On 26 May 1927, the fifteen-millionth Model T came off the production line, the event marked by a simple ceremony . . . and then Henry Ford passed the death sentence on the 'Tin Lizzy'. When the production lines finally stopped moving, some 15,500,000 Model Ts had been

From every angle the 1927 Packard Model 343 Murphy Convertible Sedan is a truly magnificent motor car. It somehow fits the scale of the country for which it was intended. This car was owned in 1978 by America's first World Champion racing driver, Phil Hill. With its superb straight-eight power unit, the Packard ranked as one of the finest cars in the world

Above: small, relatively cheap, six-cylinder
engines were the speciality of the Wolseley
company in the early '30s. The Hornet Special
sports car, of which this is a 1935 example, had
a 1.6-litre, overhead-camshaft engine producing
around 50 bhp and endowing a top speed of
almost 80 mph

A year or so after the Royale appeared, the American Duesenberg brothers, Fred and August, put *their* concept of the super-luxury car on the market, encouraged by their backer, the flamboyant Erret Lobban Cord. Advertising superlatives (which for once in an American while were justified) greeted the appearance of the Duesenberg Model J in December 1928: 'It is a monumental answer to wealthy America's insistent demand for the best that modern engineering and artistic ability can provide . . . Equally it is a tribute to the widely-recognised engineering genius of FRED S. DUESENBERG, its designer, and to E. L. CORD, its sponsor, for these men in one imaginative stroke have snatched from the far future an automobile which is years ahead, and therefore incomparably superior to, any other car which may be bought today'.

The new Duesenberg had a straight-eight twin-ohc engine with four valves per cylinder displacing 6.9 litres, with a claimed output of 265bhp at 4250rpm: the chassis, which was exceptionally rigid in construction, came in two wheelbase lengths, short (11ft 10½in) and long (12ft 9½in), although one specially commissioned limousine had a wheelbase of 14ft 10in. The standard of engineering was exceptionally high, and much use was made of aluminium in the

Preceding page: a superb 1930 Duesenberg Model J convertible sedan. The Duesenberg was one of the few American cars with a true sporting pedigree. Although Fred and August Duesenberg were brilliant engineers, it took the skills of Erret Lobban Cord to sell the Duesenberg

Right: a Duesenberg Model J boat-tail speedster, with aluminium coachwork by Murphy and the 'basic' 265bhp, overhead-camshaft, straight-eight engine
(Donald L. Carr, Yellow Springs, Ohio)

Below: a 1935 Auburn 851, equipped with a supercharged, 4585cc engine, giving a power output of 150bhp and a top speed, via the two-speed rear axle, of 100mph. Each car was hand-built and carried a plaque to guarantee that it had been tested to over 100mph
(National Motor Museum, England)

car's construction; according to *The Motor*, the Model J was the world's most expensive car, with a chassis price of £2380, while typical American convertible bodywork brought the cost up to £3450. The Duesenberg looked better when it was fitted with open, sporty bodywork; somehow more formal carriagework didn't seem to suit the chassis so well. Not so long ago the author saw a Model J *sedanca de ville* which, although undoubtedly a very fine car, looked a little too high and narrow for its length. But the Duesenberg was a successful model considering the times that it was born in, with sales averaging one a week during its production life of 1928 to 1937, and is still one of the most sought-after of all antique cars. Current price, if you can find one, of a well preserved Model J Duesenberg is approaching £60,000 . . .

Doubtless you would have to pay even more for the highly exotic Model SJ Duesenberg, fitted, as its title suggests, with a supercharger, a centrifugal blower in the American idiom, running at five times crankshaft speed and boosting power output to a claimed 320 bhp, giving the car a top speed of 129 mph (the unsupercharged J was capable of 116 mph) and the ability to reach 100 mph from rest in 17 seconds. It was not a typical American car of its

Right: a 1932–3 version of the famous SS One fixed-head coupé, with a six-cylinder, 50 bhp, side-valve engine
(Coventry Motor Museum, England)

Below: the Lagonda company produced its first V12-engined cars in 1937, in the shape of the V12 and Rapide; these were followed in 1938 by a more sporting version of the Rapide called the Le Mans, an example of which is pictured here. The 4480 cc engine, common to both models, produced 225 bhp in the Le Mans, 50 bhp more than in the Rapide; the increased power output was due to a raised compression ratio and four, instead of two, carburettors
(Stratford Motor Museum, England)

day . . . or, for that matter, any other day.

Nor, indeed, was the V12 Twin-Six Packard, whose 7298 cc power unit was silken-smooth, yet gave sizzling road performance. Introduced in 1930, this was Packard's second venture into dodecuplicity of cylinders, for they had built the original Twin-Six in 1916, and sold over 35,000 of them before production ceased in 1922. Designer of both Packard V12s was Colonel Jesse G. Vincent, who had gained his original inspiration from a V12 Sunbeam aero-engine imported into the United States just after the outbreak of World War I. This second V12 Packard lasted in production until 1939, and was bodied by the great American coachbuilders of the day; with a price tag of $4000-$6000, the Packard V12 represented excellent value for money, and a total of 5744 was built. A front-wheel-drive variant, built in 1932, didn't reach production.

Not that this was the only American V12, for Franklin, Lincoln and Pierce-Arrow announced luxury models with this engine configuration, while Cadillac, having persevered with the manufacture of V8s since 1915, brought out both V12 and V16 models during the 1930s. The other great American V16 of the 1930s was the Marmon, which had an 8-litre engine and made its appearance in 1931; to rival Cadillac and Marmon, another famous American quality car maker, Peerless, made plans for a V16, and built a prototype with an elegant Murphy body before falling sales caused them to abandon car production in 1931. Soon afterwards, however, prohibition was repealed, and Peerless resurfaced . . . as the Peerless Corporation, brewers of Carlings Ale, having decided that quenching America's thirst was a less risky business than pandering to its taste for luxury.

Nor were big V engines restricted to American manufacturers, for the Daimler company had been building their Double-Six since 1926, and continued to build it in capacities varying from 3743 cc to 7137 cc for the next decade, encouraged by Royal patronage; King George V had several Double-Sixes in his stables. Like its French contemporary, the Voisin V12, the Daimler Double-Six compounded complexity by not only having twelve cylinders but having twelve *sleeve-valve* cylinders . . .

Voisin, never noted for the conventionality of his engineering, also built a straight-twelve, again with the sleeve-valve engine that was his hallmark, while the Bucciali brothers, who used V12 Voisin engines in front-wheel-drive chassis, made a sixteen-cylinder 'Double-Huit'.

In 1931, Hispano-Suiza introduced their most spectacular model, the 9425 cc Type 68. As a publicity stunt, that great French motoring journalist Charles

233

Left: a 1934 Talbot 105, with a six-cylinder engine of 2970cc, which gave the car a top speed of more than 90mph; this model was fitted with a preselective gearbox, built by Georges Roesch, in which the lever was needed only for down-changes (National Motor Museum, England)

Right: the 1934 Graham-Paige Straight 8, which was fitted with a centrifugal supercharger rotating at 5¼ times engine speed, could reach 95 mph

Below: up to 1930, Nash concentrated on a range of six-cylinder-engined cars, but that year saw the introduction of a 4.9-litre straight-eight with overhead valves. This engine was steadily developed until 1942 and found homes under a great many different bonnets; the example shown here is a drophead coupé of 1932, with hydraulically operated hood (Château de Grandson, Switzerland)

B power unit which, incidentally, soldiered on throughout the decade in a variety of guises, surviving into the 1940s as the motive power for Spanish-built Ford trucks.

For those who could afford it, however, V8 motoring was a revelation, as *The Autocar* witnessed in 1936: 'To drive a V8 for the first time is to sample virtually a unique motoring experience. Everything that this machine does is achieved remarkably easily. It suits the laziest driving mood with its almost exclusively top-gear running abilities, as well as providing in the fullest measure a swift car for point-to-point travel when such is wanted. This car may be got moving by using first and second gears for just a few yards, and then the engine will pick up at once and pull away smoothly on the quite high top gear ratio. It runs thereafter even in slow-moving traffic and conditions that involve taking right-angle corners without the slightest need for a change-down to be made. Hills are the easiest prey to the car, all normal main-road gradients being treated as acceleration bursts if the driver wishes . . .'.

Forty years on, it's a view that can be endorsed wholeheartedly, for the author's first experience of 'the greatest thrill in motoring', as Ford advertising called the V8, was in Northern France with a 1936 Model 68 V8 which, despite the vast change in road and traffic conditions since it was built, could hold its own with most 1970s popular cars, cruised at 50–55 mph and had perfectly acceptable ride and roadholding. Yet in 1936 one could buy a fully-equipped Ford V8 saloon for just £250, a similar price to cars of only 10 or 12 hp from other British manufacturers (for by this time the V8 was built at Dagenham instead of being shipped over from Canada).

Indeed, the equipment and performance of these American cars put them in a class by themselves, even though their styling might not have wholly coincided with European taste. Some years ago, the author was talking to a motorist who had interspersed a succession of Rolls-Royces with a 5-litre Hupmobile Eight around the year 1936, and he remarked, 'the American car didn't suffer too badly in the comparison!'.

Features which we nowadays take for granted, such as radios, synchromesh gearboxes and independent front suspension, first appeared in mass-production terms on American cars.

Cheaper motoring really entered the realms previously reserved for the exotica when the straight-eight Graham appeared in 1934 with a supercharger as a standard offering. A six-cylinder version was announced in 1936, capable of 90 mph, and boasting overdrive on the upper two of its three gears; a button on the dashboard controlled the operation of this overdrive, which, when the button was pulled out, engaged automatically at speeds over 40 mph, and disengaged below 30 mph, when a freewheel came into operation.

Overdrive had first appeared in 1934 (although some earlier cars had a geared-up top speed, which wasn't quite the same thing) on that remarkable (and ugly) car, the Chrysler Airflow.

Above: when Henry Ford finally got around to authorising a V8 model, the car proved to be an enormous success, thanks once again to Ford's uncanny ability to give the people what they thought they wanted

Left: Ford advertised that driving a Ford was the greatest thrill in motoring and, arguable though that statement may be, the smart V8 was an exciting and fine car

Brainchild of Cal Breer, the Airflow's 'back-to-front' design was the result of wind-tunnel testing, and proved to be too extreme for the average purchaser, who liked a car to have a recognisable bonnet (so later Airflows had a curious 'widow's peak' grafted on to their front contours). Although it wasn't a great success, the Airflow did condition the public for the streamlines that were to come from other makers, and, in this context, it's worth noting that the wind-tunnel had become part of the car stylist's stock-in-trade relatively early on, although its use was by no means universal. Ford had developed an experimental streamlined car in their wind tunnel as early as 1930, and in 1932 used wind-tunnel techniques to improve the airflow around their new Lincoln models. In view of this, recent claims that the wind-tunnel wasn't used in the development of the Lincoln-Zephyr, the first Ford product to have a monocoque body/chassis unit, seem surprising for its shape was every bit as slippery as that of the Airflow. Developed by Dutch-born John Tjaarda under the patronage of Edsel Ford, the Lincoln-Zephyr kept the Lincoln name afloat at a time when falling sales of its more conventional models seemed likely to cause the marque to vanish from the scene altogether. Its sleek, unconventional

Below: Henry Ford's once-avowed intention of never building a V8 had evaporated by the mid 1930s, as Ford V8s maintained the marque's prodigious record of sales successes. Ford introduced the 3.6-litre V8 in 1932 at $460 and in 1935 one million were sold. This is a 1936 sedan, built in England but identical to the American product

lines even drew qualified praise from the English press: 'A certain amount of adjustment is needed as regards the unusual appearance, but from all points of view a remarkable car has been produced'.

It wasn't long before streamlining was all the rage in Europe, too; Panhard gave birth to the curious 'Dynamique', with spatted front wings and 'China-closet' curved windows at the sides of its narrow windscreen (which boasted *three* wiper blades) and grilles over the headlamps which were miniature replicas of the sloping radiator grille. The Art Deco interiors of these Panhards were every bit as eccentric as their outward appearance.

Paul Jaray's work for Maybach attracted attention, too . . . but mostly was regarded as a Showtime eccentricity: 'Reminiscent of submarine practice, the Maybach', commented *The Motor*'s man at the 1935 Paris Salon, 'with barrelled body and wings . . . the headlamps are recessed into the wings'.

With his Aerosport, which appeared at the same Salon, Gabriel Voisin returned to a theme he had successfully used on racing cars a decade before: the body as full-width aerofoil, with wheels set in the pontoon wings which formed an integral part of the design. To the eyes of 1935, the Voisin looked thoroughly odd, but then the design was a quarter-century ahead of its time;

Below: streamlining found its way on to several cars of the 1930s, and some of those models were very sleek indeed. The Peugeot 402, which was introduced in 1935 with a 2.1-litre engine, was certainly streamlined, but its body was so wide that the chassis had to be fitted with special outriggers in order to support the weight. Even the headlights were concealed behind the radiator grille so as not to cause any obstruction to the airflow, as can be seen on the 1937 model pictured here
(Peugeot collection, France)

Right : the amazing Panhard Dynamic of 1937.
It featured, apart from unique styling, a backbone
chassis, torsion-bar suspension, worm drive and a
central driving position (later discarded for the
more normal left-hand drive)

245

continued: 'If we have not progressed so rapidly in the production of this car as was done in other spheres, it is because there were two main difficulties to be overcome. First of all the requisite purchasing power had to be created and, secondly, lengthy research had to be made to produce this low-priced machine with a maximum performance for the minimum horse power. The proposed car will not only be the best, but the cheapest car in the world, and will give 100 per cent service'.

Few Volkswagens were, in fact, built before the war, and even Adolf Hitler, one suspects, might have been surprised that the car to which he had been sponsor would survive until the 1970s and become the best-selling car of all time in the process. It had been, apparently, originally inspired by one of Ledwinka's earlier designs . . .

At the same period that he was backing the Volkswagen, Hitler was also pouring money into the Mercedes and Auto-Union Grand Prix cars, to ensure Nazi dominance on the racing circuits of the world, and had ordered the construction of a system of high-speed motorways – *Autobahnen* – of which some 800 miles had been completed by 1937, at a cost of £56,000 a mile.

The construction of specially-designed motor roads had been mooted as far back as the 1890s, when schemes for a motorway from London to Brighton were published: but it took a dictatorship to introduce the concept to Europe.

Even outside the totalitarian states, the face of motoring was altering radically, with production concentrated more and more in the hands of the big battalions, who were thus able to educate the public into buying cars which were, in many ways, inferior to those they supplanted, though the new models were bedizened with all kinds of tempting gadgets. Many motorists of the 1930s were, anyway, first-time buyers, who didn't have a standard of comparison; and there was now a vast number of motorists – they were no longer an eccentric minority, for a survey taken in 1935 proved that there were some 35 million motor vehicles in use throughout the world.

Inevitably, this growth of motoring led to an increase in restrictions on the motorist. In 1936, for the first time, British motorists had to undergo a driving

Below: this straight-eight limousine was made at the height of Packard's 'classic' period in 1936. The mid 1930s were important times, as far as Packard models were concerned, because 1935 saw the first slanting radiator grille (*right*), while wire wheels, solid front axles, mechanical brakes and automatic chassis lubrication were major items which disappeared in the following year

Above and below : one of the great luxury cars, this Packard of 1939 spent its working life in Sweden with a Swedish tobacco company. Its power unit is of the straight-eight variety (Skokloster Museum, Sweden)

Right and below: the Packard 115 coupé, of 1937. This model had a great deal in common with the 120, which had been introduced two years earlier; one major difference, however, was that the 115 was fitted with a 3.6-litre, six-cylinder engine as opposed to the straight-eight of the sister car, which by 1937 had grown from 3.7 to 4.6 litres

Bottom: this 1939 Cadillac 135 bhp V8 was part of the Swedish Royal Family's collection; this actual car was used frequently by King Gustav V (Skokloster Museum, Sweden)

registered car, while in the United Kingdom the average number of people to every car was 30.6.

At the far end of the scale came China, with 13,123 Chinamen to each car . . .

Since many of the world's countries had no indigenous motor industry, there were obvious export outlets; America sold between 9 and 13 per cent of its total output to overseas customers during the 1930s, while Britain, admittedly with a smaller annual production, had increased its export sales to more than 17 per cent by 1937. The total export figure of 1936 was almost double the overseas sales made in 1933. The turning point in British car exports was apparently 1931, when Britain went off the gold standard, making English cars financially more attractive to overseas buyers. A typical example was that of Vauxhall, who in 1929 exported only 150 cars; in 1931 the figure had risen to 800, by 1932 it was up to 1750, more than doubled the following year to 3650 and in 1934 reached 6800. Of course, Vauxhall was helped by being part of the General Motors organisation, which meant that the company could take advantage of its adoptive parent's assembly plants across the world for sales and service facilities, as well as for the conversion as necessary to left-hand-drive.

Ford, of course, had assembly plants all round the world, and Rootes were also establishing footholds overseas, encouraged, no doubt, by reports like the one which stated: 'In particular, the Hillman Minx has proved a "best seller", not least because of its roominess in its own horsepower class – a point appre-

Left : the archetypal British sports car of the 1930s was the MG – wind-in-the-hair motoring without bankruptcy and with a great sporting tradition. This is a 1937 TA, with long-stroke, 1290cc, pushrod-overhead-valve engine

Right and above right : this Alfa-Romeo 8C-2300 came second in the 1935 Le Mans 24-hour race and was later used on the road by Mike Hawthorn. The car was designed by Vittorio Jano and was fitted with bodywork by Touring of Milan; its twin-overhead-camshaft, eight-cylinder engine (*above right*) gave the car a top speed of 115mph from its supercharged 2336cc (National Motor Museum, England)

Left: Daimler have long been renowned for
building large, luxurious limousines and this
Straight 8, of 1937 is no exception, with its
4½-litre engine. The example shown here was
originally owned by a Lady-in-Waiting to Her
Majesty the Queen
(Coventry Motor Museum, England)

Below: a rare example, assembled in Britain, of Citroën's famous 7 cv model, with independent suspension, front-wheel drive and unitary construction. The saloon version was long used in France by the police and was probably hardier than the convertible
(National Motor Museum, England)

Lanchester, for these two oldest of British firms had combined during the Depression. Humbler makes appealed to the humbler monarchs: Prince Mahomet Ali of Egypt had a Humber Pullman limousine, while an Armstrong-Siddeley saloon was the chosen mount of the Attah of Igbitta Lokojo, from Nigeria.

On the other hand, during 1937 Britain imported £1,515,836-worth of motor vehicles and accessories; oddly enough, considering that there were already rumours of war in the air, the only country to have increased car sales to Britain was Germany, which in 1937 sold British motorists £86,202-worth of motor cars, against £5875-worth in 1936. All other countries showed a more or less marked drop in sales to Britain.

Just imagine . . . in the Spring of 1938 the British motorist with £700 in his pocket could choose from over 400 different cars of around 70 different makes, ranging from the 7.8hp Austin Seven at £112 to the 23.8hp Talbot at £695, and there were still the expensive models like the Alfa-Romeo, Bugatti, Bentley, Autovia, Rolls, Hispano *et al*, at prices in excess of £700. . . .

This was, however, the high point of the recovery from depression: by the

Below right: a 1939 Dodge Custom 3.6-litre sedan
(Skokloster Museum, Sweden)

summer exports and imports were both in decline. In the first seven months of 1938, American cars worth £415,322 were imported into Britain, compared with £841,585 for the same period in 1937. German imports, £54,720 in July 1937, plummeted to £8708 in July 1938.

Then came Munich. Already the car manufacturing companies were involved in the setting up of 'shadow factories' for the production of war material: now the threat of war with Germany once again proved how vital the motor vehicle was to the nation. Cars were used to evacuate children, invalids and hospital patients from areas vulnerable to aerial attack; they were used to mobilise the ARP and the emergency services; they were used to transport the Prime Minister, Neville Chamberlain, to and from the aerodromes in Britain and Germany in his high-speed dash to the Four-Power Conference at Munich with Hitler, which averted the war for a year.

'And what of the private individual?' asked *The Autocar.* 'Supposing it had been necessary for London to be evacuated, then London alone had 140,000 private cars, capable of carrying, at need, some 500,000 persons, which might well have proved a vital factor in relieving other forms of transport.'

In their inimitable fashion, the British authorities rose to the occasion by discouraging people from owning cars by announcing an increase in the annual road tax from 15s to £1 5s per horsepower, and increasing the tax on petrol from 8d to 9d a gallon. This brought the amount contributed to the national purse by the motorist to £104 million, more than one-tenth of the total. Justifying the increase, which was to come into effect from the beginning of 1940, the Chancellor, Sir John Simon, showed once again that the motorist was regarded as having a bottomless pocket: 'Side by side with the reduction of income tax in 1934, my predecessor reduced the private car tax to 15s per horsepower. The users of private cars, who very largely correspond with the income tax paying classes, have, for five years, enjoyed the benefit of this reduced scale of taxation. Therefore, I feel bound to ask them, in these stern times, to submit to a substantially increased scale.'

With bland ignorance of the possible consequences of his proposals, Sir John commented: 'We ought, I am sure, to avoid any measures which would have a generally depressing effect upon industry . . .'.

Shortsighted MPs welcomed the tax on 'luxury motoring' as a means of curtailing the manufacturer of motor cars and lessening the traffic on the roads, together with the burden of their upkeep. It was as though the 19th century mechanophobe, Colonel deLaet Waldo Sibthorpe, who regarded engineers as lower than vermin, was once again stalking the corridors of Westminster to heed the development and progress of the car.

Before the tax came into effect, however, a more effective curtailment of private motoring was declared, as Britain went to war against Germany. Once again the motor vehicle, reviled in peacetime as a rich man's plaything, would prove the vital hinge on which battles were won or lost. More than ever before, this was to be a petrol war. . . .

Right: another example of a Barker-bodied Rolls-Royce Phantom I. This Torpedo-style car was once owned by the legendary Greta Garbo (Château de Grandson, Switzerland)

Below: a 1938 BMW 328 and a Bucker Jungmeister aircraft of the Luftwaffe

The quarter-ton Jeep, built by Ford and Willys, was *the* famous vehicle of World War II and did much to keep the allies mobile in the worst of conditions. *Below and right*, a model from 1944 is seen here in retirement near the National Motor Museum
(H. Schumaker Collection, England)

variety of military equipment of all kinds under the 'shadow factory' scheme. Leyland Motors, for instance, had opened a vast new engine and transmission plant, which was now turned over to making tanks, bombs and other munitions. Daimler built two 'shadow factories' near its works in Coventry; these were initially wholly engaged in the production of Bristol Mercury, Pegasus and Hercules radial aero-engines.

As the centre of so much of the motor industry, Coventry was particularly important to the British war effort. The Germans, whose anticipations even ran to having aerial photographs of important car factories available in 1939, were obviously aware of this, and their attempts to bring the motor industry to a standstill added a new word to the English language – 'Coventrated', meaning complete and utter destruction by bombing. On the night of 14 November 1940, German bombers destroyed the centre of Coventry, and the raids continued until the following April. The city had preserved much of its medieval heritage, despite its industrialisation, and many historic buildings were destroyed (although the crazy buildings in Much Park Street occupied by Lea-Francis Cars, surely the oldest structure ever used as part of a motor factory, survived).

Around 170 high explosive bombs and mines were dropped on Daimler's Radford factory, which was seventy per cent destroyed – yet production was increased, as the company had expanded into 44 dispersal factories reaching from Newcastle to North Wales.

Among the other casualties of the blitz on Coventry was the famous Motor Mills, birthplace in 1896 of the British motor industry. Daimler had moved out in the 1930s, however, and at the time of its demise the building was being used as an Air Ministry store.

Daimler's contribution to the war effort was extremely varied – gun turrets, parts for Bren and Browning guns, rocket projectors, four-wheel-drive scout cars and armoured cars, buses, and, during the final year of the war, a large Government order was received for a fleet of cars for the use of high-ranking officers once Germany had been occupied.

Other companies, apart from using their normal production expertise, also contributed to the war effort with their byproducts: Dagenham byproducts were used in the manufacture of Toluole and Xylole for explosives and varnish for aircraft fabrics, while the slag from its blast furnace was converted into Tarmac, which was used to build runways for the Battle of Britain airfields. Before the war was over, the runways and dispersal points of fifty-six airfields scattered over ten counties had been constructed of Tarmac reclaimed from the slag from the Ford furnace.

Below : the amalgamation of Armstrong-Whitworth cars and the Siddeley-Deasy company heralded the Armstrong-Siddeley car, exemplified by this 1947 Hurricane drophead coupé. The marque's reputation was for solidly built, comfortable touring cars, although in reality many had a certain sporting flavour. This model used a 2-litre, 16 hp, overhead-valve, six-cylinder engine which had originated before the war. Several Armstrong-Siddeley models – Hurricane, Typhoon, Whitley and Lancaster – were named after illustrious fighting aircraft of the parent company, Hawker-Siddeley

CHAPTER 14

Weathering the Utility Years

Victory in Europe didn't bring the expected millennium for the British motorist, for motoring was very low on the list of priorities of the post-war Socialist government – although restricting and taxing the car owner seemed to be higher up the list. New cars *were* available in 1945, but you needed a Ministry of War Transport Licence to order one, and then had to wait an indeterminate period before it was delivered (unless you had the money and the contacts to buy on the Black Market).

Purchase tax, introduced during the war to discourage the market in so-called luxury goods, remained on cars, although it was removed from household appliances, such as electric fires and refrigerators. Said the Chancellor of the Exchequer, Hugh Dalton: 'There is too much congestion on the roads at home . . . the industry should concentrate on exports . . . I have been asked to take the purchase tax off cars sold in this country, but regret that I cannot do this now. I have been told that the trade want a definite statement, and I shall give it. I cannot hold out any hope of removing the tax for some time to come . . . The motor industry and would-be purchasers of private cars in this country should, therefore, proceed on the assumption that the purchase tax is here to stay.

'I hope that the motor industry is going to export a lot more than it sells at home. There is a great block on the roads at home and great opportunities for trade abroad. There is today a sellers' market for cars, as for other British exports, in many different parts of the world, and I hope that the motor industry will fully exploit it. This is a time for exporters not only to renew contacts with old markets but to find their way into new ones – and there is, of course, no purchase tax on cars which manufacturers export. To this extent, therefore, the export trade is stimulated, as it should be'.

This was pure doctrinaire claptrap, and only Dalton's parliamentary colleagues applauded it: the unfortunate manufacturers, beset by material shortages of all kinds, coped magnificently with the order to export half their production, despite the fact that most of their products were only pre-war models with minimal updating, and had originally been designed for the peculiar requirements of the British market with no view to sales overseas. Both Government and industry were unrealistic in their view of the situation, for the manufacturers had forecast a production of 600,000 cars in the year 1947, but only managed to build 147,767: the Government set an export target of 100,000 cars for 1946, which turned out to be 80 per cent of total output for that year!

The motor industry had one particular bugbear among the ranks of the Government, and his name has become part of the mythology of austerity: ask anyone to recall the evocative images of the late 1940s, and it's inevitable that among a list that's bound to include things like snoek, whalemeat, Civic Restaurants, ration books, Dick Barton and the Berlin Airlift will be Sir Stafford Cripps.

Cripps, whose thin, bespectacled, ascetic face seemed to personify austerity, was president of the Board of Trade and later became Chancellor of the Exchequer; although he made many statements which were received with scorn by those to whom they were addressed, few of his remarks attracted more attention than his speech to the Society of Motor Manufacturers and Traders in November 1945 in which he attempted to dictate the future marketing policy of the car industry.

'We must provide a cheap, tough, good-looking car of decent size,' said Cripps, 'not the sort of car we have hitherto produced for the smooth roads and short journeys of this country. And we must produce them in sufficient quantities to get the benefits of mass-production. That was what we had to do with aircraft engines, and so we concentrated on two or three types only and mass-produced them – not a dozen different ones in penny numbers. My own belief is that we cannot succeed in getting the volume of export we must have if we disperse our efforts over numberless types and makes'.

Commented a Manchester motor trader: 'Sir Stafford Cripps has told the motor industry how to build cars; no doubt another wise guy in the Government will now show us how to sell them . . . The retention of the purchase tax will reduce the sale of new cars in Britain to negligible proportions. That means relatively few cars will have to bear the overheads of selling and distributing costs, and prices must therefore be high'.

Certainly there was no comparison with pre-war prices: the cheapest car on the British market in November 1945 was the 8 hp Ford Anglia, at a basic price of £229, boosted by purchase tax to £293 7s 3d, against its 1940 price of £140. Some post-war prices were totally unrealistic: while a Hillman Minx cost £396 17s 3d (inc PT), a Sunbeam-Talbot Ten, which was virtually identical apart from a better-finished body, was priced at a total of £620 9s 6d, which fact attracted some irony from enthusiasts.

With tyres almost unavailable and 'Pool' petrol rationed to enough for around 270 miles a month, motoring was a fairly gloomy business, and those who can remember the empty streets may well wonder where Hugh Dalton got his vision of unacceptable congestion, for car ownership was far from universal. At the end of the war there were only just over a million private cars on the road; the author can recall only two motor owners in his own fairly long street at that period, a builder who ran a three-wheeled James Handyvan and a family with an aged Morris Minor saloon which spent more time, it seemed, being pushed than running under its own power. Some mornings the only traffic was the leisurely milk cart, although he discovered the relentless onward march of progress when the milkman's horse was supplanted by an electric milk float (which broke down more frequently than the horse, and didn't know the round so well . . .).

Fortunately, one threat of State intervention in motoring proved empty – although it was a forecast of things to come . . . Late in 1945 *The Star* carried a disturbing feature: 'A people's car? State may enter motor industry. The Government contemplates entering into the motor trade in competition with the manufacturers'.

Although Americans had torn up their petrol coupons on VJ-Day, they too had discovered that the State was not finished with its interference, although in this case it was the manufacturers who were to be incommoded. Once the war in Europe was over, the American industry was granted permission to build 200,000 cars during the remainder of 1945, provided it could obtain enough of the necessary materials to do so. But raw materials were rare, and a series of wildcat strikes made them even rarer – and far more expensive. Into this situation was flung one Chester Bowles, the Price Administrator, who blandly announced that maximum prices for new American cars should be 2 per cent less than 1942 prices in the case of General Motors models (Chevrolet, Oldsmobile, DeSoto, Cadillac) while Ford, Chrysler and Studebaker were restricted to increases of 1 to 9 per cent. This meant, for instance, that a 30 hp Ford now cost the equivalent of £210, while a Studebaker was less than £225.

Complained Henry Ford II, who had taken over the running of the Ford Motor Company from his octogenarian grandfather: 'It costs us $1041 to

Above: a 1938 Hillman Minx. It was with the Minx that Hillman moved into the mass market in 1932, when the 1185cc, side-valve-engined car sold for £159. The car was improved by the addition of a four-speed gearbox before the outbreak of war and when hostilities ended it again found an enthusiastic market

Right: the American motor industry was considerably straitened after the conclusion of World War II, with a paucity of raw materials and a rigorous control on prices and production volumes. Ironically, in defeated Germany the motor industry was rapidly gaining momentum with the realisation of 'the people's car' – the Volkswagen. In 1948, Henry Ford II, who had taken over the family empire from his ageing grandfather, visited Cologne to test an early 'Beetle'

make a car . . . but we are restricted to selling it at a maximum of $780'.

Retorted the altruistic Mr Bowles: 'Mr Ford is selfishly conspiring to undermine the American people's bulwark against economic disaster', (but weren't the motor manufacturers American people, too?).

As in Britain, restrictions of this kind served mainly to bolster the sales of aged derelicts, pre-war cars often changing hands at well over their price new . . . often over the post-war price for the same model. American buyers did have the advantage that their war had started in 1942, and that therefore pre-war models were that much newer, but it was a mixed blessing, for the exaggerated styling of the early 1940s had not been to everyone's taste. A survey of American motorists in 1945 showed that most of them wanted four-door saloons, painted black, light grey or dark blue, with ample headroom, larger windscreens and side windows and – the view of 75 per cent – cars with a plain exterior finish rather than chromium-plated ornamentation on grilles, louvres and wings. Needless to say, the stylists ignored this latter remark, for this was the era of the full-width 'dollar grin' radiator grille.

One New York motoring correspondent was in no doubt about his feelings on seeing the new 1946 Oldsmobile: 'The grille has been further widened and lessened in height. The bumper is more massive and wraps further round the front wheels. Alas, the effect is more and more like some nightmare creature coming up for air from a thousand fathoms!'.

However, the fickle public bought the cars anyway . . . they liked the novelty of their cars to be restricted to mere external show, and there was no future for the unconventional, like Powel Crosley's sub-compact Hotshot, Preston Tucker's rear-engined Torpedo or a bold design proposed in 1945 by the

Alsatian motor manufacturer, E. E. C. Mathis, who had destroyed his factory in Strasbourg and escaped to New York when the Germans overran France. Mathis and Ford had had an uneasy alliance in the 1930s to produce the Matford car, but now the Frenchman had no intention of competing on the mass-production market. Instead he planned to make an 'ultra-light car, utilising plastics and weighing less than its five passengers'. He had, in fact, built some prototypes in France before the war, and such a venture would probably have succeeded in his homeland, but there was no future for it in America.

Americans didn't even trust new marques of car, for when Henry J. Kaiser, who had a formidable reputation as a wartime producer of military material, attempted to break into the monopoly of the Big Three – Ford, Chrysler, General Motors – he couldn't build up a sufficiently strong marketing network for his Kaiser-Frazer and Henry J lines, took only five per cent of the market in 1948 and faded away completely thereafter.

Although the world was car-hungry, it could still be quite finicky about its diet. . . .

Above: the Kaiser-Frazer Corporation set up shop in 1946 and soon bought Henry Ford's wartime Willow Run plant, from where they proceeded to display advanced and imaginative prototypes, with unit construction, front-wheel drive and torsion bar suspension. Alas, when the Kaiser reached the market, economics and engineering limitations had dictated conventional springing and a simple box-section frame. Nevertheless, the Kaiser is remembered as a car that was too innovative to survive in the conservative American market. This six-cylinder Manhattan, built in 1953, virtually marked the end of the line for the company

This was odd, because the public was clamouring for new cars: in fact, if you believed a somewhat equivocal comment by *The Times*, they would buy anything on wheels that was offered to them.

'In most countries today,' reported the paper, 'the shortage of motorcars is so acute that motorists exercise very little discrimination in buying a car. They consider themselves fortunate if they can acquire any new car, of any make, nationality and engine power. This partly accounts for the present demand for British small cars in the United States, where motorists normally prefer cars of high power and large body size'.

In fact, it didn't account for it at all, for the 'small British cars' which were making such an impact on the American market were cars which didn't compete with existing US models at all, and attracted an entirely different kind of customer. One British model which particularly enshrined itself in American automotive mythology was the MG TC Midget, a sports car of pre-war character which offered lively handling and quick acceleration, and could consequently run away from any large American gin-palace on a twisting road, although the larger car was very likely faster in a straight line.

Austin exported many small cars styled on transatlantic lines, although again it was almost certainly their 'nippiness' which sold them rather than Americans buying in desperation: the Austin A90 Atlantic even set up a number of American speed records, and so the old bomber factory which housed Austin's export division was kept fully occupied.

There were some curious features about the British export drive, but none more odd than the case of the Citroën factory at Slough, where components were shipped in from France, assembled into complete cars for the British market – and fifty per cent of them were then solemnly exported overseas again!

By 1950, British factories were exporting some 350,000 cars out of a total output of 522,515, although the impetus of the export drive was now beginning to fall away, partly because the countries to which Britain was exporting were now building cars to meet their own requirements, partly because the British products were said to lack reliability and to deteriorate at an unacceptable rate.

Fortunately, the old taxation system based on cylinder bore had vanished in 1947, replaced for a year by a tax of £1 for every 100cc of engine capacity, thereafter by a flat-rate tax of £10; this did at least give British designers the

Below right : Sir Alec Issigonis's first design for the Nuffield Organisation was the Morris Minor of 1948. It had a unitary-construction body and torsion-bar front suspension (National Motor Museum, England)

Below : American influence on English styling is seen in the Austin A90 Atlantic of 1950, a design strangely out of character with the Austin tradition

opportunity to design cars for world markets, although not all availed themselves of the chance.

Austerity and shortages, indeed, meant that some new designs had to remain on paper: Morris designer Alex Issigonis designed a bulbously streamlined light car with torsion-bar independent front suspension, front-wheel drive and a flat-four engine. It emerged in production form with the chassis and styling intact, but with the side-valve Series E engine of pre-war vintage driving the rear wheels through a conventional transmission. It didn't matter, however: the Morris Minor would prove to be a car with inbuilt longevity, and even after production had ended some two decades later, Morris Minors of all ages would still be a common sight on British roads.

Oddly enough, the Morris Minor had rather similar styling to the German Volkswagen, which had been put into limited production in 1945 in a factory gutted by Allied bombing, after British experts and Henry Ford II had rejected the design as having no commercial future. Commented the British: 'This car does not fulfil the technical requirements which must be expected from a motor car. Its performance and qualities have no attraction to the average

buyer. It is too ugly and too noisy. Such a type of car can, if at all, only be popular for two to three years at the most'.

This was the car that would become the most popular model of all time, with sales considerably exceeding the all-time record of fifteen million plus set up in 1927 by the immortal Model T Ford (although it must be admitted that the Model T achieved its record in far less time and in a much smaller overall market).

The end of the war had left the German motor industry in poor shape. Most of the production was concentrated in the 'Bizone' (the area occupied by British and American forces) and in 1946 only managed to turn out 9900 cars and 11,200 trucks. The Russians had dismantled most of the car companies in their zone, leaving only the old BMW works, at Eisenach, in operation, while in the French Zone, only the Daimler-Benz factory at Gaggenau was working.

In 1947, production in the Bizone was again between 21,000 and 22,000 but the following year over 57,000 vehicles were built; this was, however, little more than a quarter of the annual output from the same area in the immediate pre-war period. Most of those 1948 vehicles were needed to meet demand within Germany and the total value of exports from the Bizone amounted to only £1.4 million.

Even so, that was enough for British manufacturers to complain of the potential threat from German cars in export markets, for German cars were already making inroads in Holland, Switzerland and Belgium, where the VW was exhibited at the Brussels Motor Show in January and February 1949.

Despite steel shortages, the potential of the German industry seemed good, especially until the summer of 1948, for up to that time an exchange rate of 24 Reichsmarks:£1 was in operation for export contracts for the Volkswagen and this gave an ex-works price equivalent to £200, and a retail price on Continental markets of under £350. Contracts made on this basis were still being honoured in the early part of 1949.

In mid-1948, however, the German currency had been revalued, and the new Deutschmark was being used for contracts signed after that time, at a rate of only 11.75 DM:£1. This revaluation raised the price of the VW to around £700, and took the edge off its competitiveness, making it – for the time being – less of a competitor for British small cars.

France's concept of the utility car was the 2 cv Citroën – 'four wheels under an umbrella' – with an 8 bhp, 375 cc, flat-twin engine driving the front wheels, a project developed in secret during the German occupation, as indeed had Renault's postwar offering, the 4 cv, which had its four-cylinder engine at the rear. This was the first model to be produced by Renault after its nationalisation in 1944 – the company's founder, Louis Renault, had been accused of collaboration with the Germans and died in prison – and was nicknamed 'Cockchafer' or 'Little pat of butter' because it was painted with yellow ochre confiscated from the Afrika Korps. This was to become the first French car whose sales exceeded a million, and it was to be built for fifteen years, up to July 1961.

Overall, however, the French motor industry was ill-equipped to meet demand. Partly this was as a result of wartime bombing – the Renault works, for instance, had been badly damaged – and partly because the Germans had dismantled plants and taken the machine tools and equipment back to Germany. Even without these problems, the French industry was a sick one and had been in decline since the late 1920s, mainly due to heavy taxation on petrol and a low national average income.

Recovery after the Liberation was slow – in 1946 car production was less than one-sixth the 1938 level – and the situation was not helped by a shortage of sheet steel and tyres. There were grandiose Government plans for the industry; under this 'Monnet Plan', 1947 production was to be 396,000 vehicles. In fact, the total output was 133,100 cars and trucks. A total of 460,000 cars and 75,000 trucks was anticipated for 1951. 'It seems most unlikely that so large an increase in car production will be realised' said a 1949 industry review, and the actual results (319,881 cars and 125,774 commercials) proved that the private vehicle market was taking longer to recover than had been anticipated, despite optimistic comments like those of *L'Action Automobile* in its review of the 1949 Paris Salon, the first French show since the lifting of post-war restrictions. 'Production brilliant in conception', eulogised the magazine. 'Our cars are ahead of all others. Lightness, roadholding, suspension, fuel economy, harmony of line, aerodynamic qualities . . . these are the areas in which our superiority is most marked . . .'

A British commentator showed the view of the customers outside France: 'A noticeable drawback of French cars compared with the British is the poor quality of the finish . . . it may be doubted whether the industry is equipped, technically and financially, to withstand price competition, particularly in the smaller cars'.

In any case, technical expertise was not always a guarantee of success. The situation of Ford-France during this post-war period was a striking instance.

Above: France's estimable interpretation of the car for the people theme was the Citroën 2CV, 'four wheels under an umbrella'. It was introduced in 1948 with an 8 hp, 375 cc, flat-twin engine and, in true Citroën style, front-wheel drive. Although the 2CV grew up over the years, it never lost its essential character and even in the late 1970s, outside its native France at least, it retained something of a cult status

Right: the French equivalent of the Morris Minor was the 4CV Renault saloon. Cheap and easy to produce, it was, along with the 2CV Citroën, the 'motoring for everyone' car in France

Its factory at Poissy, just outside Paris, had been completed just before the war and largely rebuilt since, to repair considerable wartime damage. It was now Europe's most modern car factory – 'a witness to the renaissance of French industry'.

The only snag was that Poissy was producing the wrong car. The American-styled Vedette had the 2158cc Ford V8 engine, with a taxable rating of 12CV, nearly double that of any other popular mass-produced French car. Daily production in 1949 was fifty Vedettes. By comparison, the contemporary Peugeot 203, rated at 7CV, was being built at a rate of almost two hundred daily. Without a complete about-turn in policy, and the development of a totally new model more suited to the post-war French market, there was no way of saving the Poissy operation. Ford weren't prepared to make that kind of investment, and in 1954 sold Poissy to Simca, who had made their debut in 1934, building small Fiats under licence.

Simca – the name stood for '*Société Industrielle de Mécanique et Carrosserie Automobile*' – had begun operations in the old Donnet-Zedel factory at Nanterre and within less than two years were among the five biggest French constructors. Their post-war offerings included the Simca-8 (available with either 6CV or 7CV four-cylinder power units), the Simca-6 and the Simca-8 Sport, an elegant open two-seater whose price (880,000 francs) was twice that of the basic Simca-8, but still attractive for such a limited-production vehicle.

It was proof, too, that the day of the specialist producers of '*voitures hors série*' was drawing to a close, for out of all those companies – Delahaye, Delage, Hotchkiss, Salmson and Talbot – only Hotchkiss, justifying its slogan, '*le juste milieu*' and Salmson could come anywhere near the price of the Simca-8 Sport, and that with rather dull-looking saloons.

Talbot, whose competition-developed Lago-Record and Lago-Grand-Sport were the most expensive models on the market, attempted to move into a more 'popular' price bracket with the 15CV Lago-Baby, fitted with a 2.7-litre four-cylinder engine instead of the 4.5-litre six used in the big Talbots. As the Lago-Baby cost a hefty 1,198,000 francs, its appearance could only delay the inevitable demise of the Talbot company.

Nevertheless, there was still a limited market for very costly special-bodied cars and there were no fewer than thirteen *carrossiers* exhibiting at the 1949 Salon, among them such great names as Antem, Chapron, Figoni et Falaschi,

Below: styling gone quite mad. This Cadillac had a body by the French coachbuilder Saoutchick

Franay, Leturneur et Marchand, Pourtout and Saoutchik. Their elegant vehicles, however, were no more typical of the future of the French industry than was the curious little voiturette built at St-Denis by De Rovin. This was, if anything, even more utilitarian than the 2CV Citroën, with an open, two-seater body, like that of a dodgem car, and a 425cc flat-twin engine. With an output of only five to six cars a day, the Rovin was scarcely competitive . . .

Italy's biggest manufacturer, Fiat, was concentrating on economy, too, with the post-war version of their 500cc Topolino ('Mickey Mouse') and its larger 1100cc and 1500cc sisters.

The Italians had great hopes for their car industry. 'Since the end of hostilities', wrote *l'Action Automobile*, 'the Italians have had the wish to give their car industry once again the maximum of gloss, for they will largely rely on it to give, at one and the same time, prestige in foreign markets and an economic renaissance for their country'.

The quickest way to gain prestige was of course, in competition, and many of the post-war Italian cars had been developed in sporting events. Alfa Romeo, Maserati, Cisitalia and Ferrari had all won international events in the late 1940s, successes reflected in models like the Ferrari 166 Mille Miglia or the supercharged 2.5-litre Alfa Romeo Super Sport. Even so, these prestigious marques took only a tiny percentage of a market dominated by Fiat. Experimental models like the front-wheel-drive Caproni and the rear-engined V8 Isotta-Fraschini Monterosa stood no chance at all.

Other countries seemed to play little part in the picture of world car production in the late 1940s. 'The use of motor vehicles in Japan has never been extensive', noted a 1949 report. 'The mountainous character of the country and its poor roads have made it dependent chiefly on shipping and railway facilities for long-distance traffic. There were only 140,000 civilian motor vehicles in 1941, of which 64,000 were trucks'.

The Japanese motor industry did not become significant until the mid-1930s, when production rose almost five-fold in three years, thanks to the Motor Car Manufacturing Enterprise Act of 1936, which cut taxes on motor manufacturers and set up protective tariffs. Three companies – Nissan, Toyota and Datsun – dominated the industry and employed some 21,000 people between them.

They came through the war without direct bomb damage and by 1946 were producing over 14,800 vehicles annually, almost all of which were commercials. By 1947, production had risen to almost 19,500, of which only 1700 were cars:

Below: Sydney Allard created magnificent cars described as 'motor cycles on four wheels'. This is a 1950 J2, which is powered by an Arden-Mercury V8 engine of 3917 cc (National Motor Museum, England)

Japan, it seemed, would never become a force to be reckoned with . . .

Czechoslovakia, now behind the Iron Curtain, was nevertheless still exporting to the West, mainly to Belgium and Holland and, following a 1949 trade agreement, to Argentina. The country's four export offerings were two Tatra models, the big V8 and the four-cylinder Tatraplan, both of course air-cooled; the Skoda 1100, with its backbone chassis; and the little, two-cylinder, 615cc Aerominor, which achieved success in its class in the 1949 Le Mans 24-hour race.

Sweden, after a flurry of activity during the war years, had dropped to an annual output of 6500 vehicles – less than the 1938 total. Most of those 6500 were built by Volvo and only 2300 of them were cars. The Philipsen company, which had assembled American and German cars before the war, introduced small cars to replace the German models in the late 1940s. The country's 1948 exports were of little significance on the international scene, totalling only 650 cars and 2000 commercials.

So the 1940s came to an end, with Europe concentrating on economy and America exuberantly extravagant. Automotive engineering was certainly moving forward: unfortunately good taste was heading in the opposite direction and, whatever else the fifties might be remembered for in the automobile industry, restraint was not on the menu.

CHAPTER 15

The Flamboyant Fifties

Above: despite styling similar to that of many pre-war American motor cars, the Jowett Javelin was rather different underneath, with its flat-four engine; unfortunately, the car-buying public thought it was too radical, so it was not a great success; nevertheless, 30,000 examples were manufactured
(National Motor Museum, England)

Above left: one of the first British cars to move away from the economy vehicles of the late 1940s and early 1950s was the Ford Consul; this is a 1955 drophead coupé version
(National Motor Museum, England)

Left: three famous works MGs. They are Y-type 1½-litre saloons of 1953, seen here at Carlisle during the Daily Express Rally

Right at the beginning of the 1950s, the British motor industry was staggered by a merger which was more of a shotgun wedding than a marriage of convenience, bringing two great rivals together. William Morris had become Lord Nuffield, but had now lost interest in the empire he had created, and was finding increasing solace in his prolonged cruises to Australia; his former lieutenant, Sir Leonard Lord, now headed Austin and had once sworn that the only reason he would return to Morris would be to take it apart 'brick by bloody brick'. But Austin and the Nuffield Group did merge to form the British Motor Corporation, although there was little rationalisation of model ranges, and the old Austin-Morris rivalries seemed to persist. The group's share of the market, originally about fifty per cent, began to slip steadily downward.

Of course, this may have been due as much to the fact that the rest of the British motor industry was catching up technically as to any residual bitterness between Nuffield and Lord: Ford introduced its first truly modern range in 1950 with the Consul, with an ohv four-cylinder engine, hydraulic brakes, independent front suspension and integral body/chassis unit, and followed this soon after with the similar, six-cylindered Zephyr.

'Judged both on performance and on value for money, the Zephyr is a very satisfactory car,' commented *The Autocar*. 'It is quiet yet lively, roomy without being cumbersome, and it had a quiet modern line without the vulgarity often produced by the addition of excess ornamentation.' The test concluded with a masterly piece of ambiguity: 'It goes and stops and handles well'.

Soon after this, Ford announced a unit-constructed small car, the 100E Anglia, whose 1935-designed power unit was also used in a remarkable survival from the Mesolithic age of motoring, the Ford Popular, the cheapest real car on the British market, whose styling dated back to 1937. It was produced in the old Briggs Motor Bodies factory at Doncaster, which meant that manufacture of bodywork for the unorthodox Jowett Javelin had to stop: and Jowett ceased car production. Remarkably, the crude little Ford Popular remained in production until 1959.

Unfortunately the new-look Fords seemed to attract the attentions of the gadget-lover, for above all the early 1950s were the era of the bolt-on gimmick: amber plastic bug-deflectors in the shape of birds decorated the bonnet top, chromed masks sat like eyelids above the headlamps, windscreens were given overhanging peaks like the eyeshade of a Hollywood newspaper editor, 'portholes' lined the bonnet. Bad taste was rampant.

It was, it seems, the efforts of the motor industry to come to terms with the new technology that resulted in many of the styling gaffes of the early 1950s; that, plus the determination of the mass producers that their products should not look *too* different from their competitors. Describing the 1954 Earl's Court Motor Show, *Autocourse* commented: 'The post-war tendency to add more and more chromium plate to a previous year's model and then to present it as new and original was continued, and it would seem that for the "middle line" of transport, at least, fashion has settled down to a common shape . . . the discerning eye will not find this shape offensive, nor for that matter will it greatly please . . . many manufacturers have simply scaled down their more commodious brainchildren into, for example, the Austin A30, the Fords Anglia and Prefect, the Fiat 1100 and the Standard 8. This shameless copying is hardly stimulating . . .'.

There were still, however, nationalistic tendencies; some of the 'upper crust' British manufacturers were still using the razor-edge line in their bodywork, though this rather ugly design feature had a *passé*, 1930s, air to it. Italy, noted a contemporary journalist, 'enjoyed the charmingly elegant fantasies which made a nonsense of any close collaboration between pure engineering and design'; France 'concentrated on voluptuous curves'.

However hard the manufacturers tried, the praise always seemed to be qualified: 'The Frazer Nash hard-top also has a plainly defined radiator intake, though the effect is partially offset by the quasi juke-box adornment on the carburettor intake' . . . 'on the Lancia Gran Turismo the glass is recessed, giving a somewhat clumsy effect', and so on.

Below: the styling of the 1950 Ford Popular, in essence, dated back to 1937, but this was cheerfully overlooked by the buying public on the grounds that the 'Pop' was the cheapest real car then available on the British market. Remarkably, it survived with few changes until 1959

Above: by American standards of the early 1950s, when bad taste was rampant in the automobile industry, the design of the 1956 Ford Fairlane might even be considered conservative

Perhaps, too, the spirit of the age was shown in the adoption of brighter paint and trim schemes. After the war, most car interiors were trimmed in a dull brown; by the early 1950s, more colourful seats and fascias were in demand and bright synthetic plastics gave the opportunity to provide interior design colour-keyed to the overall paint scheme of the car. Not that this was always in very good taste . . . two-tone finishes became popular on many saloon cars, and metallic colours were increasingly used, including some particularly nasty shades of green. One 1955 Rolls-Royce appeared in two-tone orange and cream, while the 1954 London Show saw a flamingo-pink Triumph!

Nowhere was bad taste more evident during this period than in the United States. American cars smirked their way into the 1950s behind chromium-plated radiator grilles of surpassing vulgarity: they ended the decade with front-end styling reminiscent of the head of some deep-sea fish and tailfins like rocket-powered guppy. Nor is the piscine analogy far-fetched, for a promotional film made by Ford of America around 1956 showing a car stylist at work, bathed in a dim, religious light, emphasised that he took inspiration from natural forms – like a tank-full of tropical fish. Then the film showed this Renaissance

man take up his pencil, as though he were a medieval monk about to illuminate a psalter – and design a futuristic car that was as impracticable as it was repellent. Fortunately this was a flight of fancy that was not about to be launched on an unsuspecting public.

'Cars of the future' were very much in the corporate minds of the American motor moguls in this period, although quite why is something of a mystery, save that their appearance at motor shows did go some way to accustoming the public to the shape of cars to come – a sort of cushioning against bodyshell-shock.

Cadillac started the tailfin vogue in 1950, the modest kick-ups at the tips of the rear wings acting as something of a relieving touch to the ponderous styling of the new models, which were the first Caddys to sell over 100,000 in a year; the fin vogue reached its peak on cars like the 1959 Buick LeSabre, on which these lethal-looking appendages were half-a-car long.

For America, the 1950s began badly, with the outbreak of the Korean War; yet this major international disturbance had little effect on the sale of motor vehicles, which that same year exceeded 8,000,000 for the first time ever (6,665,863 of these were cars).

Despite their excesses of styling, American cars were all pretty much alike

Left: the famous Mercedes-Benz 300SL 'gullwing' of 1957; this car had what was probably the nearest thing, in a production model, to a true space-frame chassis, made possible by the high sills and the lift-up doors

Below: seen at the 1952 London Motor Show, this Bentley R-type had bodywork by Freestone & Webb

underneath: most had V8 engines of around 100 hp, with six-cylinder power units reserved for the lower price ranges; suspension was generally by independent coils at the front and leaf springs at the back; sealed-beam headlights, radio and heater were regarded as virtually indispensable. On models with manual gearboxes, a steering-column gearchange made room for three on a bench front seat, but removed all precision from the operation of changing speed. The provision of a column change, with all its complex linkage, must have been extremely costly compared with the simplicity of the 'stick shift', especially to an industry reputed to count the cost of every washer.

There was an alternative, however, and motorists were prepared to pay extra for it. Automatic transmission, which had made its first tentative appearances in the 1930s, was now reliable enough to be put into mass-production. The fact that many of the early automatic boxes only possessed two forward speeds was immaterial, for those big V8s made up in torque what they lacked in economy.

One of the first manufacturers to go automatic was Buick, who in 1950 became the fourth manufacturer to achieve sales of over half-a-million cars in a year – and nearly 430,000 of these were fitted with the new Buick Dynaflow

Above: perhaps the most famous of all motoring flops was the Edsel, a car which showed just how fickle public opinion could be. The market which millions of dollars worth of planning had foreseen for the new car flatly rejected it and in two years only 35,000 cars were sold. This is a 1960 Edsel Ranger, from the cheaper end of the range and the marque's final model year

Left: the AC Greyhound used a 2.2-litre Bristol engine, front disc brakes and coil-spring/wishbone suspension. It was similar in basic outline to the Ace and Aceca models, but had a larger, four-seater coupé body on a slightly longer wheelbase

Below: Citroën's DS19 caused a sensation when it was announced in 1955, setting standards of aerodynamic efficiency by which others were to be judged even into the late 1970s. The car used hydraulic power for brakes, steering, clutch, gear engagement and suspension trimming, but thanks to its outstanding efficiency a 1.9-litre, four-cylinder engine was quite enough to endow sparkling performance

torque-convertor transmission. Madison Avenue outdid itself in coining names redolent of speed and power for these early automatic transmission: 'Tip-Toe Hydraulic Shift with Gyrol Fluid Drive', 'Hydra-Matic', 'Powerglide', 'Ultra-Matic', 'PowerFlite'.

It was definitely marketing, not engineering, which sold cars in the America of the 1950s: in fact, these Rockets and Firedomes and Silver Streaks were only in their element on the dead-straight turnpike highways, and under more demanding conditions their road-holding deficiencies were emphasised to the full. However, the great marketing dream turned to a nightmare in 1959 when Ford introduced the Edsel, designed after thorough market research, and discovered that public taste could be expensively fickle. The motorists for whom the Edsel had been designed failed to buy it, and production was curtailed inside two years, with only 35,000 cars sold. The marketing men had failed to anticipate a move away from large cars, an error of judgment that cost Ford an estimated $250,000,000.

By the end of the decade, America was definitely warming to the compact, partly to combat the success of imported European cars, which were introducing American drivers to new standards of economy and roadholding (and if you can remember just how vague the steering was on some European small cars of the late 1950s, you'll get some measure of the directional imprecision that the average American monster of the epoch must have possessed).

Mind you, America's idea of 'compact' was a long way from Europe's concept of small cars. Oldsmobile and Buick entered the field late, in 1960, with a 3.5-litre V8 power unit which was to be adapted for the British Rover later in the decade. Oldsmobile's F85 compact was 15 ft 8 in long, two or three feet longer than the average medium-sized European car.

Europe, though, didn't have the advantages of wide-open spaces and cheap petrol which had encouraged Americans to think big (though growing urban congestion was showing the US industry the disadvantages of this policy); imported petrol and, on the Continent, taxation systems which penalised large engines, had conditioned Europeans to regard the optimum size for a power unit as being below 2 litres. Citroën's advanced and sharklike DS19, introduced in 1955, for instance, was a big car in everything but engine size. Despite having hydraulic power for steering, brakes, clutch operation, gear engagement and suspension trimming, the 22 cwt DS had a four-cylinder power unit of only 1.9 litres, relying on its slippery shape for efficient speed.

If the DS represented a practical production version of the 'car of tomorrow', across the Channel Rover were developing a futuristic vehicle which stood little chance of seeing any sort of production; unlike the American 'dream cars', however, this car was *avant-garde* in its engineering rather than simply in its styling. Its secret was its power unit – a gas turbine. Rover had pioneered this method of propulsion as far back as 1946, when they began work on the world's first gas-turbine car, 'JET 1'. A second prototype was built in 1955 and this had a rear-mounted gas turbine in a normal saloon body.

Towards the end of 1956 Rover unveiled the 'T3', using a compact gas turbine developed from Rover's IS/60 industrial power unit, half the size of JET 1's engine. A heat exchanger helped to keep fuel consumption within reasonable limits – in a track test, the T3 returned 13.8 mpg at a steady 40 mph, and 12.8 mpg at 80 mph.

While the T3 was the first practicable Rover gas turbine car, the company warned: 'This model is in no way a final design, representing only another stage in Rover gas turbine development. There are still several problems to be solved, both in respect of body style and engine arrangement, before a truly operational car can be produced'.

The main advantages of the gas turbine engine were its excellent power-to-weight ratio, and the absence of radiator, clutch and gearbox. In the T3 the engine was mounted at the rear of a two-seater saloon body made from glass fibre, with wrap around windscreen and large rear window; because of the engine's high torque to weight ratio, the specification included four-wheel drive, with a De Dion axle at the rear. Rover were to persist with their gas-turbine development programme for some time but the power unit never found

Left : a toothy grin from a 1950 Buick perhaps sums up what the car designers in America were doing at that time

Right: one of the most popular British sports saloons of the 1950s was the Sunbeam-Talbot; this is a 1954 example (Coventry Motor Museum, England)

Below: Jaguar's XK 140 was not only a magnificent sports car in terms of engine and chassis, it was also well styled; the XK series has become one of the most revered sporting lines ever built

its way into a production vehicle. The only practical benefits to the Rover customer lay in refinement of engineering specification on piston-engined cars and a subsequent styling study on a jet chassis that formed the basis of the 2000 saloon of the 1960s.

In the year of the introduction of the T3, Europe had been given a salutary reminder of the finite nature of petroleum resources in the wake of the Suez War when the fuel supply routes were closed and fuel rationing had to be imposed. There followed a brief period of happy hitch-hiking for the majority of the British public, those without transport being given lifts by those who could get petrol. By careful choice of which vehicles you waved your thumb at, it was possible to extend your motoring experience in the most intriguing way. On one day during this adventurous period, the author rode in (or on) vehicles as diverse as a mid 1920s Sunbeam tourer and a window cleaner's ex-WD BSA motor bike!

Even when the rationing was over, there was always the thought that it could happen again, and manufacturers and the motoring public suddenly began to take seriously a new breed of cyclecar which had, indeed, begun to appear before Suez, but was then regarded as something of a joke. One of the first such cars was the Isetta, a strange device like an Easter egg mounted on a roller skate, powered, if that is the appropriate word, by a rear-mounted 245 cc engine with only one cylinder.

It was followed by the Heinkel, a similar vehicle (similar enough for the two makers to go to law about design resemblances) with a 198 cc engine capable of returning 86 mpg and propelling the vehicle at over 50 mph on the level.

Their shape naturally earned these little creatures the nickname 'bubble cars', although their makers liked to think of them as 'cabin cruisers'. One of the strangest was the little Messerschmitt Kabinenroller, built by the erstwhile German aircraft manufacturer; this had tandem seating for two moderate-sized adults and a child under a plastic cockpit cover. It had handlebar steering and a 191 cc Sachs two-stroke engine which had to have its direction of rotation reversed to achieve a 'reverse gear'. There was also a supersports version of this car, the KR500 Tiger, which had a 500 cc engine and four wheels instead of three, as obstructions like manhole covers were liable to upset the roadholding of the original model.

The bubble-car vogue was a short-lived one, for these little cars were noisy, cramped and not over-reliable, although at one stage in 1960 the British-built Scootacar was, at £275, the cheapest enclosed car on the market (it looked rather like a perambulating phone box and was built by the Hunslet Engine

Below: JET 1, seen here preparing for a demonstration run at Silverstone, was the world's first gas-turbine-engined car; it was built by the Rover company in 1946, but although Rover continued to produce gas turbine prototypes, and racing cars, culminating in the T3 of 1956 they never satisfactorily solved all the problems which prevented the gas turbine being put into volume production

Above: the mid 1950s had their own share of economy models. This is an Isetta Moto Coupé, commonly referred to as a 'bubble car'

Right: this is the 'supersports' version of Messerschmitt's strange Kabinenroller, the Tiger. Inside and out, the cockpit bore more than a passing resemblance to that of one of the company's more familiar aircraft (National Motor Museum, England)

roomier Cortina, which appeared in 1962 after the space in the Ford range between the Anglia and the Consul had temporarily been plugged by two short-run 'stop-gap' designs, the Classic and the Capri, and which, selling in similar price ranges to the little car, proved its most serious competitor.

'You've never had it so good' was the political slogan which ruled the Mini's natal year, and indeed 1959 had seen an unparalleled crop of new designs; apart from the Issigonis baby, there had been the Triumph Herald, designed by Harry Webster, the Aston Martin DB4GT, 6¼-litre V8 light-alloy engines for Rolls-Royce and Bentley, the Ford 105E Anglia, the Daimler SP250 (a rather ugly glassfibre-bodied sports model), the MGA 1600, the Sunbeam Alpine, Hillman Minx with Easidrive automatic and new models from AC and Armstrong-Siddeley.

There was another slogan which was soon to affect motoring in America, however. Chevrolet had broken away from tradition to produce the Corvair compact, which had a flat-six air-cooled engine mounted at the rear and swing-axle independent rear suspension. Its unfamiliar handling characteristics led to a crop of accidents and a book written by a crusading lawyer, Ralph Nader. The book's title? *Unsafe at Any Speed* . . .

Right: a 1963 two-door Chevrolet Corvair Monza convertible. The Corvair was a brave effort to break with American tradition, using a rear-mounted, air-cooled, flat-six engine and independent rear suspension by swing axles. Any hope that might have been had of changing the style of the American automobile was comprehensively destroyed by Ralph Nader's safety-crusading book, *Unsafe at Any Speed* – a damaging indictment of the Corvair's design

Left: Ford's answer to the Mini was the mechanically conventional, if visually imaginative, new Anglia, introduced in 1959 and available with 997 and, later, 1200 cc engines. The Anglia's most striking feature was the backward raked rear window, supposedly designed to resist rain and road grime. With the Cortina, the Anglia laid the financial foundations for cars such as the Capri and Fiesta, which were to follow

Right: a 1956 Armstrong-Siddeley Sapphire is typical of the British luxury motor car of the 1950s, with very conservative styling

Below: this 1952 Lea-Francis London Motor Show car is a 2½-litre sports model, which used a 2496 cc, four-cylinder engine. It could reach a top speed of 102 mph, by courtesy of its 125 bhp power unit (Stratford Motor Museum, England)

who the author used to visit regularly, offered a choice of vintage Bugattis at under £200 each, a Siddeley Special tourer for £90, a Fiat 501 two-seater with a dickey full of spares at £60, and so on.

Breaker's yards were still places of romance, not the dreary eyesores full of spavined, rusting, totally useless monocoque bodyshells that assault the eye nowadays. Brooks of Edenbridge, Goodey of Twyford – these were names to be conjured with in the early 1960s, though they were already a vanishing breed. Their mounds of obsolete spares played a considerable part in the motoring economy of those days, helping to keep the many orphan vehicles still in use – Beans, Swifts, Crossleys, Trojans and a host of other quadragenarians – in running order.

Even the mass-producers expected *some* skill of their customers, for the large majority of popular cars had no syncromesh on bottom gear; although the gearchange may have been rubbery and vague, it still helped to know how to double-declutch . . .

There were many reasons why the car changed from being a glamour symbol to what it had been in America for many years – a necessity of life. True, the Americans tricked out their cars with styling gimmicks, but that was to induce the motorist to change his car for a later model on grounds of fashion, even though its utility was unimpaired.

One reason why Britons, especially in rural areas, began to place more emphasis on car ownership, was almost certainly Doctor Beeching's celebrated 'Axe', which closed down uneconomic railway branch lines all over the country. Bereft of reliable public transport, country dwellers were forced to become motorists if they wanted to travel. The growing network of motorways helped, too, enabling journeys to be made at speeds rivalling those of the fastest express trains, in greater comfort and convenience and from door to door as well.

There were great changes in design: the early 1960s saw the last of the mass-production side-valve models, although only a few years earlier this configuration had dominated the popular car field. The last of the side-valves were both – originally – Ford designs, although only the 100E Popular retained its parentage, and used a power unit whose basic design dated back to the early 1930s. Of equally venerable origin was the V8 engine of the Simca Vedette, basically the 22hp 'Alsace' power unit designed for Ford-France in 1935, and taken over with that company's Poissy factory when Ford stopped building cars in France in 1954. Those had been among the first power units designed for international, rather than narrow national, markets. Now there was great cross-fertilisation of ideas and components between the car-producing nations.

Surveying the decade's first Earls Court Show, in 1960, the motoring press noted that the exhibits included 'British Vauxhalls with an American automatic gearbox, a Swedish Volvo which is shortly to be built in Birmingham, and has a Scottish-made body of Italian styling, German Borgwards with Hobbs automatic gearboxes from Britain, French Facel Vegas with American V8 engines, Italian Ferraris, Lancias and Maseratis with British disc brakes . . .'.

As yet, however, there was little sign that the big multi-national corporations like Ford and General Motors would use their international expertise to produce a range of vehicles of common design, with parts interchangeable across Europe. The concept of personal mobility hadn't advanced that far. A Vauxhall was still a Vauxhall, with very little in common with its German sibling, the Opel; and the same went for British Fords and German Fords, where even the basic technology differed, with the British favouring rear-wheel drive, the Germans front-wheel drive. It was a very wasteful way of utilising a European organisation, with two lots of research and engineering being used to produce dichotomous model ranges aimed, ultimately, at similar market sectors.

Yet it had not always been so. In the early 1930s, Fords had followed the same design across Europe, with the little Ford 8hp Model Y being built in Britain, France, Germany and Spain. That pioneering venture had been immured behind the protectionist tariff barriers erected by the nations of Europe during the depressed years of the 1930s, and the model strains had been developing in

Below: a classic sports car, the Pininfarina-designed Ferrari Dino 246GT. The Dino, named for Enzo Ferrari's son, was introduced as the Dino 206 in 1965, going on general sale in 1967. The engine capacity was increased from 2 litres to 2.4 litres in 1969 – bringing the designation 246GT. 195 bhp from the mid-mounted V6 give the car a top speed of 148 mph and acceleration from rest to 60 mph in around 7 seconds. Exceptional roadholding, handling and braking make the Dino a truly outstanding driver's car

isolation for three decades, their national differences accentuated by the war.

Then Ford of America made a massive cash bid, which brought Ford of Britain entirely under their control. However, fuelled by successful models like the Anglia and the Cortina, Ford was in expansive mood, marked by the construction of a modern headquarters building costing several million pounds at Warley in Essex in 1963, and the opening of a new factory at Halewood on Merseyside the same year. Halewood, representing an investment of some £70 million, was a major step in a policy of decentralisation which created, in effect, production lines several hundred miles long, engines from Dagenham being shipped to Halewood and the truck factories at Langley and Southampton by special trains, and gearboxes from Halewood and back axles from Swansea being moved cross-country by the same method. This was theoretically the best interpretation of Henry Ford I's dictum that a factory must have the best possible transportation links. Stoppages at one factory can disrupt national production however.

There were complaints from some political quarters that, with Vauxhall owned by General Motors, the new set-up at Ford brought half the British

Left: Chrysler's small car for the 1960s was the Hillman Imp, a diminutive, rear-engined saloon distinguished by its splendid, if fragile, all-alloy, four-cylinder, 875cc engine. The Imp first appeared in 1963 and was followed by the Super Imp, as shown here, and Singer and Sunbeam variants

Left: for many people the Ford Capri, which the company introduced in 1969, was the answer to a prayer. Its '2 plus 2 coupé' styling made it a sports car for the man whose family had outgrown the sports car, but whose wallet could not support a grand tourer. Once again Ford had filled a glaring gap in the market. The Capri could be had with engines ranging from the four-cylinder 1300 to the 136 bhp, 3-litre V6, and with a wide variety of trim packages

Above: in 1964, Volkswagen obtained control of the Auto Union group from Mercedes-Benz and a year later the disused Audi name was revived. The 1½-litre Audi 60, shown here, joined the 80, 90 and 100 ranges in 1968, to give the company a stylish and technically impressive spread of models

Above right: a 1964 Alfa Romeo Giulia Berlina saloon. In common with many other manufacturers, Alfa Romeo were no strangers to the art of clothing the same mechanical basics in differing styles of bodyshell to produce ostensibly different cars. The Giulia succeeded the 1300 cc, twin-cam Giulietta in 1962 and was offered with 1570 cc engine, disc brakes and a five-speed gearbox

industry under direct American rule; there was little justification for such anxieties, however, for, quite apart from the fact that both Ford and Vauxhall were left to operate as virtually autonomous units, producing cars specifically designed for their own markets, the massive cash resources of their respective parent companies were used to finance the building of new factories, and thus the creation of many new jobs. It was during the early 1960s that Vauxhall built a new factory at Ellesmere Port, also in the Merseyside development area, to produce a new version of its 1-litre Viva model.

It was American cash which was to prove the salvation of the Rootes Group which, having just opened a Scottish factory to build its new rear-engined Imp light car, found itself in financial trouble, and needed bailing out. With Government approval, the Chrysler corporation took a £27 million stake in the company in 1964, and three years later put in another £20 million; the final takeover came in 1973.

As for the other two big companies in the British market, these began the Sixties as rivals and ended the decade as a unity. For seventy years, the groups which were now known as the Leyland Motor Corporation and the British Motor Corporation had been rolling along like corporate snowballs, gathering company after company, although by the mid 60s both seemed to have run out of inertia. The last act of rivalry was the acquisition of Jaguar in 1966 by the BMC, which gave the corporation an entrée into the prestige-car market; shortly afterwards, Leyland bought Rover to prevent BMC from having it. Even during the 1950s, the economic signs pointed towards a merger between the motoring giants, and a succession of Managing Directors, including Leonard Lord, Joe Edwards, Sir William Black, Sir George Harriman and Lord Stokes, had paved the way for the eventuality. In association with the Labour Government's Industrial Reorganisation Corporation, Leyland and BMC considered a rescue operation for the ailing Rootes Group. This was not a commercially sound proposition and Rootes was acquired by Chrysler. The Government-supported concept of a British corporation large enough to compete with the increasingly sophisticated continental manufacturers was sufficient to create the basis for the merger, which took place, not without considerable difficulty and bitterness, in the February of 1967. The company is still evolving through rationalisation of model ranges and streamlining of internal administration procedures, and is now the second largest automotive company in Europe.

Against the understandable complexity of the BLMC range, the other big European companies relied on simple model ranges of perhaps three or four distinct types: small, medium and large. Sporty cars gained sufficient variety to appeal to the mass of car-buyers by offering a wide range of trim and equipment, so that two identical bodyshells could leave the factory, one as a basic spartan model designed for fleet use, the other as a comfortable limousine with, for instance, wooden door-cappings and a high level of interior appointment.

From such companies it is therefore possible for a customer to choose, within the options offered, the size of car, performance, degree of sophistication and accessories to suit his own requirements.

The only real exception to the rule that a big company should keep its range simple seemed to be Fiat, which in the mid 1960s had a basic lineup of eleven different models, but as the company had a virtual monopoly of the Italian market, with something like 75 per cent of total sales, perhaps they could afford to be a little profligate in their marketing.

On the other hand, Volkswagen, who during the decade joined the Mercedes-Auto-Union group, found that stark simplicity had its drawbacks, too. At the start of the 1960s, the old VW Beetle was still selling strongly, backed up by enthusiastic press reports of its durability, but technical progress during the decade began to leave the Beetle behind – it was, after all, a child of the '30s – and Volkswagen began tentatively to diversify, offering models with the same basic layout but modern styling, although with hindsight these 'modernised' VWs seem to have dated far more quickly than the Beetle.

The unfortunate Beetle was one of the victims of Ralph Nader's *Unsafe at any Speed* campaign, although it seems that the crusading American lawyer was over-emphasising his arguments to gain the maximum of publicity. Especially in America, the motor industry and the legislature over-reacted, and the environmentalist lobby, boldened by the success of its onslaught, moved in for the kill. Figures were issued claiming – although exactly how such things could be measured was unclear – that, annually, motor cars emitted 60 million tons of carbon monoxide, 12 million tons of hydrocarbons, 6 million tons of nitrous oxide, a million tons of sulphur oxide . . . and a million tons of 'smoke'.

These arguments were given some credence by the freak atmospheric conditions prevailing around Los Angeles, where atmospheric pollution can form a dense smog layer over the city, although the inhabitants' predilection for using a car to go even the shortest distances, and to regard anyone actually seen

Right: after some three decades of building the 'Beetle', Volkswagen's association with Auto Union, perhaps helped a little by the power of Nader's *Unsafe at any Speed*, prompted the company to diversify its designs. The first 'conventional' Volkswagen saloon, the K70, appeared in 1970, inherited from NSU. It was a front-wheel-drive saloon with a water-cooled engine in 75 or 90 bhp options and was, in essence, a more universally acceptable version of the NSU Ro80

walking as some kind of freak, did not aid the situation.

Politically, there were easy pickings to be made out of the situation, and Senator Ed Muskie put a bill before Congress proposing that exhaust emissions from a motor vehicle should be 95 per cent clean before they were released to the atmosphere. This virtually meant that the exhaust gas had to be purer than the air sucked into the carburettor, but it sounded impressive, and soon manufacturers were attempting to meet this impossible standard by fitting all kinds of 'de-toxing' devices to ensure that engines ingested all their own harmful waste-products. Needless to say, power units did not benefit from their coprophagous diet, and performance and efficiency deteriorated. So much underbonnet equipment was needed to meet these requirements that Ford's engineering laboratories jokingly announced that the standard test to see whether a European Capri converted to meet California emission laws had all the appropriate plumbing was to empty a bucket of water over the engine. If any ran out underneath, there was sure to be something missing.

Having now forced the makers of all cars sold in America to conform to a standard intended to beat freak weather conditions, the environmentalists launched a campaign aimed at the additives included in fuel to promote more efficient combustion. Tetra-ethyl-lead, which had permitted increased engine

Above: NSU was another element in the Volkswagen Audi conglomerate of the early sixties and its chief claim to fame during the period was through its licensing of and experimentation with the Wankel rotary engine. The Wankel Spyder, an open version of the Sports Prinz, powered by a single-rotor, 60 bhp engine, became the world's first rotary-engined car – introduced in 1963 and going into production in 1964. The fuel crisis of the early 1970s sounded the death-knell for NSU's Wankel project, whose forte had never been good fuel consumption

Above: the Mercedes-Benz 600 was presented as the world's most automated production car. It was introduced in 1964 and used a 6.3-litre, fuel-injected, V8 engine, self-adjusting pneumatic suspension, with dampers which were adjustable while in motion, automatic transmission, power steering and electric window lifts. It also offered powered central door locking, a power sunroof, power-assisted boot and bonnet lifts, and a powered passenger compartment division. The whole was clothed in a huge, long-wheelbase limousine body

compression – and hence efficiency – when it was first put on the market at the end of the 1920s and regarded as a miracle additive and personified by a Betty Boop-like character called Miss Ethyl, was now reviled as a causer of brain damage, and plans made to phase it out.

Engines thus became less competent at burning their fuel, petrol consumption went up and in a world increasingly aware of the finite nature of its oil reserves, could one argue that the environmentalists were proposing the right solutions?

Many of these environmental lobbyists seemed to be non-motorists, misunderstanding completely the role of the car in society, and instead of encouraging manufacturers to produce cars with impeccable steering, braking, roadholding and acceleration – cars which were safe to *drive*, a criterion which the majority of manufacturers were already aiming at – they forced through legislation to ensure that a car was safe to *crash*!

In order to be able to sell in many markets, therefore, manufacturers nowadays have to spend vast sums of money in deliberately writing-off brand-new cars in carefully controlled crashes to prove the integrity of the passenger compartment. One particularly regrettable aspect of the situation was that the environmentalists succeeded in killing off the mass-produced convertible

in America at the beginning of the 1970s, as open tops were dangerous in the unlikely situation of a car being inverted. It apparently did not occur to these people to insist on the standardisation of roll bars.

One expensive blind alley followed by manufacturers in response to such hostile lobbying was the 'Safety Car', various concepts of which were built in America and Europe in the early 1970s, and most of which succeeded in looking like high speed bulldozers. Heavy, clumsy and inelegant, it seemed that the only thing that they could do successfully was to run into solid obstacles!

Mark you, some of the manufacturers seemed to have brought trouble on their own heads: the early part of the decade had seen American car makers, who had earlier mutually abandoned the 'horsepower race', suddenly burst forth once again with advertising extolling the power and speed of their products. Sherwood Egbert, President of Studebaker (which was fast approaching the end of its long life of vehicle manufacture), announced his company's 1963 models with the fatuous boast: 'If the customer wishes to buy more horsepower than he can use, he will be able to buy it from Studebaker'.

However, the new emphasis on performance did have some worthwhile results: of the new generation of American cars, some were destined to become classics, like the Ford Mustang, which set new records for first-year sales, and the Anglo-American Ford GT40 sports-racer, which won Le Mans four times in a row. Pontiac pioneered the use of a cogged-belt-driven overhead camshaft among American mass-producers on their 1966 Tempest range. Hitherto, this means of driving an overhead cam had only been used by the small, German, Glas company.

Another unusual model introduced for the 1966 season was the Oldsmobile Toronado, with front-wheel drive; the Toronado's running gear was used, a year later, on the Cadillac Eldorado, an 18ft 5in long 'personal car' which re-introduced, in vestigial form, the famous (or infamous) Cadillac fins, although these were now evident at front *and* back . . .

General Motors made quite a notable contribution to the British motor industry in 1965, when they agreed to let Rover take over the discontinued Buick-Oldsmobile-Pontiac, 3.5-litre, V8 alloy engine, which gave an extra boost to Rover's car range, going into production in 1966.

It was not, however, a happy year to introduce a high-powered new model to the British market, for the Government had decided to hit the motor industry hard. Purchase tax was increased by ten per cent, road tax went up by sixteen per cent, hire purchase conditions were stiffened; yet the British road user was already contributing over £1000 million in taxes to the Government – eleven per cent of the total national revenue. The effect on the motor industry was 'chaotic', and the result was a crisis which saw redundancy, short-time working and a drop in sales.

Commented Sir Patrick Hennessy, Chairman of the Society of Motor Manufacturers and Traders: 'It is hard to reconcile the situation with the

Government's avowed intention of helping industries of high productivity and export performance. Last year (1965) the British motor industry's exports reached £785 million and represented sixteen per cent of our total visible trade. Yet this industry, whose success overseas is so dependent on volume in the home market, is – once again – being forced to bear the brunt of Government economic policy.

'Government researchers have estimated that the country loses hundreds of millions of pounds every year because of the sheer inefficiency of road congestion – but the Government says we cannot afford to save that money. Is this the new way ahead? Every industry has to move every day materials, parts and supplies, using expensive sluggish transportation and meeting inevitably with congestion and inefficiency on arrival at the docks. So here again we are not competitive – particularly on the Continent.

'Instead of export exhortation, suppose we built some roads from the industrial areas to the docks: what a practical contribution that would be! But we are told we cannot help exports in that way unless we sacrifice hospitals and schools. A red herring – and an unpalatable one at that. Sooner or later, we in

Left: the Hillman Imp was the basis for this small sports car built first in Essex and then in Lincolnshire. It is the Ginetta G15

industry have to tackle this road problem. It isn't only a motor industry problem child. All the nation's industries know that roads are a continuation of their manufacturing processes and supply costs, and it is now evident that until they join together in a national effort, we shall have no effect on Government'.

Although many major road-building programmes were instituted during the 1960s, the constraints on the use of cars were multiplying with equal rapidity. For instance, in 1965, Britain's new non-motoring lady Minister of Transport announced that as a temporary experiment, a nationwide maximum speed limit of 70mph would be instituted. It gives some idea of the credence that can be given to a politician's concept of 'temporary' when one considers that fourteen years later, that 70mph maximum was still in force in spite of almost constant lobbying for its reappraisal.

Since then, the cancer of overall speed limitation has spread to most countries, either as a result of fuel economy measures or because of the attitude of the safety lobbyists. The facile argument that 'speed kills' is not really defensible, because the majority of drivers keep to self-imposed limits, and the faster driver is normally more aware of what is going on. It's the slow, half-asleep

Below: a 1965 Saab 96; unveiled in February 1960, the 96 featured a redesigned rear end grafted onto what was otherwise virtually the same shell as the 95. The 96 also used the same 841cc, 38bhp two-stroke engine as the 95 but had more luggage capacity, more passenger room, a new instrument layout, new ventilation system and a larger fuel tank. It was an immediate success and, even with the opening of Saab's new factory at Trollhättan, the company could sell all the cars it could build. Eventually, the two-stroke engine was ousted by a 'cleaner' four-stroke V4

motorist who often causes accidents by his total oblivion of what other road users are doing. But of course when an image of 'responsibility' for such exponents of creeping paralysis has been created for political ends, one can hardly accuse those slow drivers of being a menace to the more rapid drivers on the road!

Faced with such unreasonable legislation, and fearing that the situation could only deteriorate in the future, the keener motorists began to seek solace in the ownership of cars built in happier days, whose driving required some little skill and which, in short, made driving within the limits still bearable. During the 1960s, therefore, demand for veteran and vintage cars grew apace, and prices began to rise. Unfortunately, the increase in value of such vehicles also attracted the 'investor', who just saw an interesting car in terms of its potential increase in capital value, and was prepared to salt it away and rarely, if ever, use it. The activities of such gentlemen priced many of the true enthusiasts out of the market, and forced them to look to more recent cars of interest for their recreation.

Left: a Rolls-Royce Silver Shadow, photographed in August 1965, just prior to the model's public announcement. The styling found favour with the company's discerning clientele and the new Shadow was a resounding success. The 6750cc, V8 engine, as is traditional in a Rolls-Royce, has 'adequate' power and gives the car a top speed of almost 120mph

In that context, when one looked back on the 1960s, one realised how very few truly classic designs had appeared in that decade. Maybe the future held something better?

CHAPTER 17

The Seventies and Onward

Left: the Jaguar E-type caused a sensation when it first appeared, in 1961. It offered 150 mph performance at a modest price and in a sleek and elegantly styled package, which looked fast even at a standstill! The car was launched with the 3.8-litre, six-cylinder unit, but this was finally superseded by the magnificent 5.3-litre, V12 engine in 1971, the year in which this Series III roadster was built

With the decade almost over, the 1970s were revealed as one of the most dramatic episodes in the history of motoring, with the motor industry lurching between optimism and despondency as the victim of international politics which at one stage seemed to threaten its entire future.

The 70s opened well enough for the British industry, although Ford, Vauxhall and Chrysler all had their share of industrial unrest. By 1973, optimism was the keynote.

Reported *The Times*: 'The fruits of a bumper 1972 are already being reflected in plans for 1973. The Society of Motor Manufacturers and Traders says that the British industry is geared to produce 2,500,000 cars and car sets (for assembly overseas) this year. This compares with 1,900,000 last year. Mr Gilbert Hunt, the society's president and also chief executive of Chrysler UK, talks of a four to five per cent rise in home demand and a twenty per cent rise in exports . . . Much is at stake for the country's biggest earner of foreign currency this year'.

Mr Hunt's optimism was, however, misplaced; at the end of 1973 the Arab–Israeli War erupted, bringing the Arab oil embargo in its wake. For maybe half a century, there had been forecasts that one day there would be problems in obtaining Middle East oil: faced with the reality, European governments instituted all kinds of restrictions, from limits on the amount of petrol that could be bought at one time to car-less Sundays. Most of these measures were mere windowdressing, introduced to bring home the seriousness of the crisis to the general public, for cars used only a tiny proportion of oil imports, the bulk being used by industry and public services.

Far from rising, British sales fell by almost 200,000. Soaring raw materials prices and wages caused new car prices to rise at an alarming rate – nearly 40 per cent in a year in some cases – and savage taxes were placed on petrol to curb demand.

The worst of the oil crisis was soon over, but it left a vastly changed motor industry in its wake. The salvation of British Leyland, faced as it was with massive losses, lay in the hands of the government, and the company was 'taken into public ownership'. Whilst it is arguable that such a drastic step might not necessarily be certain to increase the company's commercial efficiency, there is little doubt that without Government intervention at the time, Leyland would look quite different today. Chrysler, too, was in trouble, although as it was an American-owned company, the British Government could hardly take it over as it had British Leyland: but again millions of pounds were handed over to keep Chrysler in Britain.

To an outside observer, it might have seemed like unfair preference; after all, the other British motor companies were trading in the same market. But both Ford and Vauxhall, using shrewd marketing and attractive model ranges, actually increased their share of overall sales, Ford, indeed, nudging the British Leyland makes (lumped together for statistical purposes, although still market-

Top: the body style which carried Aston Martin into the 1970s; this car is a DBS Vantage

Above: the Fiat 126 replaced the ageing but still much loved 500 in 1973. With the adoption of a slightly larger, 594cc, engine (albeit still with only two cylinders) and a completely revised bodyshell, the 500 continued in spirit if not in substance. With 23 bhp on tap, the 126 would reach 65 mph and would travel close to sixty miles on a gallon of petrol. Even at this end of the motoring spectrum, there is a call for a touch of creature comfort and Fiat catered for it with this version of the basic 126, the Personal

Left: Ford were late into the proliferating market for the small hatchback car, but when their contender, the Fiesta, finally arrived in July 1976, it soon found acceptance in the very discerning market place. The Fiesta was launched with a choice of 957cc or 1117cc engines, later supplemented by a 1300 option, and it followed many competitors in using front-wheel drive

Above: TVR of Blackpool have concentrated on sports cars and, in their brief history, on one basic design of car, although a major variant was added in 1978 when a convertible joined the range. During its time of production, that basic design has evolved steadily to keep up with the times. This is a 1969 Vixen with a specially tuned 1650cc Ford Cortina engine

ed under their old marque names) out of first place during the early part of 1976, although Leyland made efforts to retaliate.

There were, indeed, doubts about the government's understanding of business management: the civil servants didn't always seem to be pulling in the same direction as the Leyland management. As witness the announcement by Whitehall in September 1976 that British Leyland was planning to invest some £100 million on the development of a successor to the Mini. As this car wasn't due to be put on the market for another three to four years, the announcement was premature to say the least, and broke all the industry's normal rules of confidentiality over forthcoming models. The press reported that the Leyland directors were 'furious', and that the leak had caused a drop in the sales of the current Mini. There were also doubts about the economic viability of such a model, as all the leading European companies were already active in this area of the market, known to the manufacturers as the 'B' car class.

The main problem with building small cars – and the fuel crisis had really only advanced a swing to such economical vehicles – is that a great deal of them needed to be built before they become financially attractive. After all, the plant and labour costs are virtually those of a larger car, the only saving being on metal and other raw materials.

Ford solved the problem neatly by building their Fiesta in three strategically-placed factories; at Dagenham, at Saarlouis in Germany and in a new, purpose-built plant at Almusafes, near Valencia in Spain, where Fiestas would be built not only for the booming Spanish market but also for other southern European countries. The necessary raw materials could therefore be bought in quantities sufficient to keep these three factories supplied, the 'economies of scale' meaning that components could be purchased or produced at the minimum unit cost. Typical of the new generation of small cars, the Fiesta was a two-door model with hatchback tailgate, and offered a wide range of options and trim – even a luxury Ghia model. Small no longer meant 'austere'.

The launching of the Fiesta in 1976 also proved a new truism: in order to think small, a company had to be very big. And, in general, the climate of the 1970s was inimical to the limited-production, specialised manufacturer. Aston Martin almost vanished and Jensen *did* vanish; only those specialists like Rolls-Royce or Morgan who catered for a readily identifiable minority of well heeled motorists could face the future with some assurance.

In fact, the period was marked by huge groupings, both national and international, either as straight commercial mergers, or as looser comings-together where companies retained their independence but pooled resources for the development of some technical resource, such as a new design of power unit. Typical of the latter type of arrangement was the Comotor company, formed jointly by Citroën (who were owned by Pardevi, a Swiss company owned 51 per cent by Michelin, 49 per cent by Fiat) and by Audi-NSU (who were a subsidiary of Volkswagen); Comotor, whose factory was in the Saarland, produced Wankel Rotary engines, a type of power unit which seemed to hold out possibilities of being more easily adapted to meet American exhaust pollution levels. Just to complicate the merger picture still further, by 1976

Citroën had come under the control of the privately-owned Peugeot company (which for a decade had been operating a joint research, development and investment programme with the state-owned Renault company!). First fruit of the Peugeot-Citroën alliance was the Citroën LN minicar, referred to in the French press as 'a little lion with Javel sauce', which used a two-door Peugeot 104 bodyshell and a 602 cc, flat-twin, air-cooled power unit and transmission from the 3 cv Citroën.

Above: the NSU Ro80 was the second car to feature Felix Wankel's rotary-engine design, the first being the rare NSU Spider. The front-wheel-drive Ro80 also featured a three-speed manual gearbox, with a torque converter and a clutch operated by a touch-sensitive switch in the gear lever knob

Left: in spite of being subject to one of the longest waiting lists for delivery anywhere in the motor industry, the Morgan Plus 8 still maintains the Morgan tradition of open-air motoring with few compromises. The Plus 8's 3½-litre Rover engine endows the car with anything but vintage performance, 0–60 mph being possible in 6.7 seconds

Right: the Jaguar XJS, seen in automatic form, used the 5.3-litre V12 two-cam engine first seen in the last E-types. Not only did the XJS have magnificent acceleration and top speed (155 mph), but it was one of the quietest tourers ever available. The XJS, despite its conservative instead of *avant garde* styling, represented motoring of the 1970s: sophisticated, silent, quick and expensive, a far cry from the chugging and puffing vehicles that graced the roads (or tracks) of the motor-car age in its infancy

Above: Rolls-Royce turned to Pininfarina of Turin to design the coachwork of their top of the range car, the Camargue, which was introduced in 1975. The resulting shape was not to everyone's taste, many people thinking the car less elegant than the Fiat 130 Coupé to which it obviously owed its basic line. Mechanically, the Camargue relied on the 6750cc, all-alloy, V8 engine

Right: in the 1970s, Citroën produced the CX series which was as futuristic as its predecessor, the DS. Here is a CX2200 Pallas

So the new generation of cars for the late 1970s were really quite conventional restatements of established themes. Comfort, of course, was greatly improved on the majority of them, and features like heated rear windows, servo-assisted disc brakes became common standard fitments; but most of the refinements were relatively minor ones. Faced with the reality that motorists were changing their cars less frequently, manufacturers began using phrases like 'the long-lasting car', and Porsche came up with a car that would 'last for twenty years' (although as there were still fifty-year-old cars in daily use, one felt that they could have been a little more ambitious). Such trends caused the prophets of the automotive future to trade in their crystal balls for utility models.

In 1966 the *Wall Street Journal* looked ahead to transportation in the year 2000, and forecast a 'dazzling, Buck Rogers-like world of plush, electronically controlled ground vehicles and 6000-mile-an-hour airliners'.

Ten years later, their view of the future was more cautious: 'Today's airline passenger or motorist should be able to step into a vehicle of the early 21st century and feel right at home'.

Coupled with this attitude was that of the protagonists of public transport, who wanted to drive people away from the privately-owned motor car and force them to use what Americans called 'mass-transit vehicles' – buses and trains. But these were no longer economically viable alternatives to the car: however expensive owning a motor vehicle had become, public transport had become more expensive still, and with services pared to a minimum, especially in rural areas, the use of public transport became only a desperation measure for many people.

Politically-biased 'consultation groups' talked grandly in their big brotherly way about increasing the cost of petrol still further so that the motorist would be frightened out of his car and on to the public transport by the 'perceived cost

Above: the 1978 Citroën LN, a Peugeot 104 by any other name, was an example of badge engineering, European-style, brought about by the polarising of the industry during the 1970s

Left: a 1973, 8.3-litre Cadillac Eldorado, which has everything either automatic or power operated. This front-wheel-drive car even has lights that come on automatically when the daylight fades

Right: the 1977 Porsche Turbo, with turbocharged, 3-litre, flat-six engine, clearly demonstrates its lineage from the company's 911 series, which was launched in 1964 and gradually treated to more and more power and the essential aerodynamic and chassis changes to cope with it. The 3-litre Turbo had truly spectacular performance, with sixty miles per hour attainable from rest in just 5.2 seconds

of his journey'; but what they seemed unable to comprehend was that for the family motorist the car would always win. On a train and bus four travelled at four times the cost of one, but in a car, four travelled at a quarter the cost of one. Nevertheless, the pressure groups continued to press for cars to be abolished, despite opposition from many people.

When, in 1975, Henry Ford II was called to testify before the US Joint Economic Committee, he was questioned persistently about his attitude towards Federal aid to the car industry to enable it to make the 'inevitable' conversion from building motor cars to building mass-transit vehicles.

Commented Mr Ford: 'That's one problem we at Ford are not worried about. The real mass-transit system in the United States is the Highway system and the automobile, which are responsible for more than 80 per cent of all trips to work and all trips between cities, and for more than 90 per cent of all trips within cities. The automobile business is now about 75 years old. Most of the United States has been built within that period, and the building pattern has been made possible by the unprecedented convenience, flexibility, comfort and low cost of motor vehicle transportation.

'Even if it were possible, the United States has better things to do with its resources than build a 19th century transportation system – and then build a 19th century country so that we can somehow make do with primitive transportation.

'There is room and need for better public transportation in many places. But better public transportation will take few people out of cars and probably will not even halt the long, steady decline in public transportation usage. The few new rapid transit systems built in recent years all have drawn their riders from buses, not cars. They can be built only with enormous outlays of public funds, and generally can be operated only with additional large subsidies to cover the

growing gap between revenues and operating costs'.

What, however, of the car's alleged over-use of non-replaceable fuel and raw materials? The latest statistics available in 1976 showed that the known recoverable reserves of petroleum totalled 660,000,000,000 barrels, enough for some 34 years. And much of the world's surface remained undrilled – ninety per cent of all the oil and gas wells ever drilled in the world had been drilled in the United States. Other potential fuel sources included oil shale, tar sands, coal and organic waste matter: it seemed as though the internal combustion engine would be around for a long time yet. And 80 per cent of the materials used to build a car could be recycled to build new cars.

Meanwhile, governments were understandably taking a parsimonious look at their oil imports. In America, Congress decreed late in 1975 that the average fuel economy of all cars produced in a year by each manufacturer should rise in stages to 27·5 miles per (US) gallon by the 1985 model year, representing a 100 per cent improvement over the fuel consumption of 1974 models.

'To achieve so big a change in so huge an industry in so short a period,' claimed Henry Ford II, 'we must start right now and we have little time to

hesitate or change direction along the way'.

The motor industry world-wide, it seemed, was entering a period of unusual uncertainty, although there was evidence that the public was becoming tired of excessive government interference in their freedom to buy and use motor vehicles. Henry Ford II summed up the problems ahead in a speech to the Automotive World Congress at Dearborn, Michigan, in July 1976: 'Outside the United States, will the trend towards government control and ownership of auto companies continue, and how far will the march towards social democracy go? How will world trade in motor vehicles be affected if manufacturing and marketing are increasingly aimed at protecting jobs and generating export income rather than profits? Can private, profit-orientated enterprise survive in anything like its present form in the face of growing support for such measures as worker participation in management, compulsory profit sharing and compulsory distribution of stock to workers and unions?'.

By the beginning of 1978, the future for the motor industry seemed a good deal brighter than it had done in the period immediately following the oil crisis. Car sales in Western Europe, which had overtaken America as the biggest producer of motor vehicles at the end of the 1960s, looked set to exceed ten million for the first time. However, overall production was not quite back to 1973 levels, and it was unlikely that that year's record of 11,250,000 cars would be equalled for some time.

A main cause of this was the tremendous inroads made by the Japanese into the markets traditionally served by European manufacturers. In the late 1960s, the European industry regarded Japanese cars as a source of humour, and certainly as no sort of threat to their livelihood. Although Japanese cars *had* been technically retrograde and stylistically dreadful, things were changing.

Above: Mazda were only a matter of weeks behind NSU with their introduction of a rotary-engined car, the RX3 model being revealed in 1973. The engine was equivalent to a reciprocating engine of 1964cc and produced a useful 110bhp. While NSU struggled with their Wankel development programme, Mazda's version went from strength to strength and appeared to overcome many of the problems

Above: once Volkswagen had broken away from the constraints of a 'Beetles only' policy, they began to produce a splendid series of cars, including the Scirocco, the Golf and the Polo. The front-wheel-drive Polo was available with 895cc and 1092cc engines. This is a 1976 example

Left: having taken the two-wheeled world by storm in the early 1960s, Honda turned their attentions to the manufacture of cars and, after a hesitant start with several motor cars in miniature, they gained acceptance with cars such as the Civic and this 1977 Accord

Below: another challenger from Japan to the medium sized car market sector was the 1970 Toyota Crown De Luxe sedan. Like all Japanese cars the Toyota offered a comprehensive list of standard equipment within the basic price

From 1966, Japanese manufacturers invested heavily in development of new designs, even to the extent of buying styling packages from the Italians.

By 1970, Japan had soared into second place among the world's motor manufacturing countries and was ever eager for new markets to conquer. Already Japanese imports had made a considerable impression on the West Coast of America, but Europe felt itself safe from invasion. Japanese cars represented only a tiny fraction of total sales and as late as 1970 an eminent British motoring journalist could write: 'By the time import duty has been added to the enormous cost of transportation halfway around the world it is quite obvious that no model designed to be competitive on, say, the West Coast of America can possibly hold its own on the home ground of one of the manufacturers it is thrashing into the ground out there in the export territories'.

Japan's marketing philosophy, however, was vastly different from that of the European companies. Typically, the Toyo Kogo company, makers of Mazda cars, operated their own shipping line of some sixty ships to deliver cars to export markets, and operated on the basis that when there was a slump in home market sales, exports were to be doubled, so that overall sales volume should remain constant.

It was tactics like this which put Japan into the big league. In 1977, Japanese manufacturers were selling a million cars a year in the United States, and had six per cent of all new car sales in Europe, including over ten per cent of the British market.

Indeed, the British industry had requested Japanese manufacturers to restrict imports and claimed, in 1977, that the Japanese had agreed to keep their share of the British market down to the 1976 level of 9.4 per cent. The 1977 Japanese penetration of 10.6 per cent came as something of a shock, therefore, reinforced by the news that at the beginning of 1978 their share had risen to 13 per cent, and the Japanese industry association told the British Society of Motor Manufacturers and Traders that it would no longer give any undertaking – official or unofficial – that it would restrict UK sales during 1978.

Perhaps the Japanese industry had become too export-based for its own good. European manufacturers had attempted to move into many overseas markets by setting up local plants, thereby creating local employment; press reports accused the Japanese of exporting unemployment along with their cars. With Japan now selling almost a quarter of the world's cars, it seemed that they had reached a level of tolerance beyond which stringent curbs would be enforced.

European experts claimed that the Japanese had made a major tactical error by choosing to supply major overseas markets solely by export, rather than utilising local manufacture, and that, especially in the Third World, nationalistic demands for local assembly plants would increasingly threaten those exports.

The doors seemed to have been closed against the Japanese buying into an existing European company. They had made advances when Citroën was in trouble, before that company merged with Peugeot, but the French Govern-

321

ment had prevented any takeover from occurring. Any chance of Chrysler releasing idle production capacity to Mitsubishi (in which it held a fifteen per cent share) seemed likely to meet with a similar fate.

Faced with a dramatic fall in the car exports essential to its economic success – twenty per cent of Japan's manufacturing activity was centred on the car industry – the Japanese industry was seen to be planning for the change. Forecasts indicated that Japanese companies would shift an increasing percentage of their resources into truck manufacture and could be competing strongly on a global scale in the commercial vehicle market by the 1980s.

Another factor which was seen likely to slow down the Japanese growth was the rising value of the Japanese currency, which added to the cost of their cars.

Some indication of future trends was given by Honda's decision to open a motor cycle factory in the United States in 1979, with plans to follow this by a car factory which would be in production by 1981.

It was a policy already followed by Volkswagen, who began building cars in the United States in the spring of 1978, with plans to open another factory at a later date. Currency fluctuations played a major part in the VW decision: any manufacturer setting up operations in widely scattered countries seeks immunity from the fluctuations of the currency market. Moreover, it is possible to even out labour costs, so that the expense of building cars in a high-wage country, which can represent a considerable hindrance to an export-seeking manufacturer, could be countered by further production in low-wage countries.

The 1970s saw several of the larger manufacturers moving eagerly into the less developed countries. Fiat was one of the more interesting examples. Aware of the problems which could arise from its dependence on the relatively small Italian market, in which it held a dominant share of new car sales, Fiat diversified within Italy so that less than half its industrial energies were concentrated on car production. The company moved into new fields, like tourism and hotels, and expanded existing technologies such as aircraft production.

Outside Italy, Fiat held thirty per cent of Seat, the Spanish car manufacturer, in partnership with the Madrid government, and sold production know-how to Poland and the USSR, who set up huge car plants to produce cars based on obsolescent – in Western terms – Fiat designs. The size of these ventures can be gauged from the fact that in 1976, Lada, the Russian end of the deal, turned out 740,000 cars, virtually equal to Leyland's 1978 output.

In April 1978, Fiat and Seat joined forces in a venture to establish an Egyptian motor factory in conjunction with Egyptian financial and motor engineering interests, although at the same time it was reported that Seat was developing its own design of sports car for the Spanish market, so as to reduce the amount of royalty payments due to Fiat.

Another North African country which went out of its way to attract European motor manufacturers was Morocco, which by 1978 could count several vehicle plants in the Casablanca area, most recent of which was a Renault component factory which – with the agreement of the French trades unions – supplied items such as mirrors and seat belt anchorages to Renault-France factories.

Further afield, Third World countries were eager for the benefits that the motor industry could bring: Korea had its own car producing plant, Vietnam was courting European car companies with attractive financial concessions, Volkswagen was still producing the old Beetle in Brazil, after production of this best-selling car of all time had stopped in Europe, in volumes which made it Brazil's biggest car manufacturer.

Within a very few years the emphasis of car production had changed radically, and the chances were that it would undergo still more dramatic changes in the years ahead. Volume production, distribution networks, service and model rationalisation would be the keys to survival for hard-pressed manufacturers. It would be essential that parts for a car produced, say in Australia, should be interchangeable with those of an identical model produced half a world away.

The motor industry is now ninety years old, and in its lifetime it has transformed the face of the world more than any other. The problem now is: can the industry survive the social changes it has itself instigated?

Right: the 1975 American Motors Pacer has a futuristic body housing the traditional American package of V8 engine, three-speed transmission and independent front/non-independent rear suspension. Drum brakes are considered adequate to restrain a 4228cc top-of-the-range engine

Far right: the Citroën GS continued admirably the Citroën tradition of superior front-wheel-drive engineering and outstanding aerodynamic efficiency. Flat-four engines of a mere 1015cc or 1222cc, give maximum speeds of up to 94mph with remarkable fuel economy, in the region of 40mpg

Below: the only American sports car in production in the 1970s was the Chevrolet Corvette Stingray, this being a 1973 7.5-litre automatic

CHAPTER 18

Whatever Next?

Right: the first example of Lotus's 'up-market' cars, the Elite. This is a luxury four-seater with a highly efficient, four-valve, twin-cam engine and possibly the best roadholding and handling of all front-engined road cars ever built

Left: the styling of Leyland's Triumph TR7 did not prove universally popular, but the car itself was a solidly built, ultra-conventional medium priced sports car, with outstanding roadholding and handling and a reasonable turn of speed. The TR7 was powered by a 2-litre, four-cylinder engine derived from the Dolomite saloon. Successes in rallying were gained in 1978 by TR7s fitted with the 3½-litre Rover V8 engine, giving a pointer to the way many people hoped the roadgoing car would develop

It is certain that the present industrial groupings which make up the car industry as we know it today are going to be very different in appearance in the 1980s. One eminent market analyst predicted in 1978 that by the early 1980s the companies that would succeed in the world market were those which could show an annual production of two million cars and achieve viable sales in North and South America, Europe and Asia-Pacific. Only Ford and General Motors were in that league in the late 1970s, although the Volkswagen group was coming up fast, with Chrysler, Datsun, Fiat, Honda and Toyota the other companies considered as having a chance of achieving successful world status.

It was also forecast that new world groupings could be formed out of failing companies, just as General Motors had been decades earlier. British Leyland, for example, might become part of such a grouping and companies which already had collaborative arrangements might move closer together: Renault and American Motors might possibly combine, for already Renaults were to be built for North America in AMC plants.

Another expert saw other companies becoming one: Renault and Peugeot-Citroën, he thought, would have merged by 1985, as would Volkswagen and BMW in Germany and Saab and Volvo in Sweden. Inevitably, too, the amount of state interest in the motor industry would increase.

If the industry was going to be so vastly changed, it seemed as though the cars it would build in the 1980s would be not so very different from those it had designed for the late 1970s. The flights of fancy that had been so common in the 1950s and 1960s found themselves grounded with fatigue cracks. The hovercars, linear induction vehicles and similar devices were elbowed out by a new generation of more practical dream cars. Cars were now being conceived from the standpoint of efficiency and wind-tunnels were a standard part of the equipment of any self-respecting motor manufacturer, who used the data they provided to make his cars slip through the air with the minimum of resistance – and hence the maximum of fuel economy.

Indeed, so advanced had some manufacturers' aerodynamic techniques become that by 1978 it was becoming a real possibility that a lightweight vehicle could be constructed that would achieve a genuine one hundred miles per gallon under road conditions – after all, Shell held an annual contest for specially-built one-man experimental vehicles that were capable of one *thousand* miles per gallon under carefully-controlled conditions and although these machines were totally impracticable as a means of transport, nevertheless they did prompt some careful examination of fuel consumption criteria for more conventional machinery.

For as the 1980s came nearer, it was obvious that the car of the future would use an internal combustion engine of some kind, simply because the alternatives were in some respect or other unsuitable.

Manufacturers were, nevertheless, investigating alternative forms of power. Steam and electricity had been tried and found wanting at a very early stage in

Above: one of the most promising alternatives to the conventional internal combustion engine is the Stirling engine, a modern development of a concept originally devised by a Scottish clergyman in the early nineteenth century. This is a cutaway of the Philips 4-235 Stirling engine, showing one of its four cylinders and its rhombic bottom-end drive

Left: high-efficiency variations on the reciprocating internal combustion engine theme continue to abound. One of the most interesting is the Abingdon-Cross rotary-valved radial engine, using Cross rotary valvegear and a Baker eccentric crankshaft. The volumetric efficiency and mechanical losses inherent in the design are so favourably disposed that an output of 140 bhp from a 1600 cc production unit is a realistic projection

the development of the motor vehicle, although there were persistent attempts to revive the electric car, at least for urban use. All one could say of the electric vehicles of the 70s was that until they could surpass the performance of their Edwardian forebears, and until some revolutionary lightweight battery could be perfected at a moderate cost, they would never be a viable rival to the petrol engine. The pollution from an oil-burning electric generating station could amount to more per electric car than anything emitted by a petrol vehicle's exhaust.

More promising, perhaps, was the Stirling engine, a modern development of a 'hot-air' power unit originally – and appropriately – devised by a Scottish clergyman in the early 19th century; the 1970s Stirling operated on a closed-cycle 'hot-gas' system of some complexity, but was remarkably unfastidious in its dietary requirements. The Stirling, claimed its protagonists, could run on any fuel from peanut butter to nuclear energy with equal efficiency, and by the mid-1970s Ford were running Stirling-engined cars on their proving grounds, while a Stirling engined bus had been built in Holland.

In the early 1970s, various forms of rotary power unit had been mooted, but

Below: Renault's Basic Research Vehicle, as exhibited in London in 1974 is in many ways typical of the vehicles built by every major manufacturer as mobile test beds for new ideas in safety, styling and new, energy saving technology

Right: whatever the details of individual interpretations, the underlying theme for the future seems to be 'build small'. This is a Ghia 'City Car', shown on the Ford stand at the 1978 Geneva Motor Show. It has an overall length of just over 8½ feet and could carry four adult passengers and their luggage. The futuristic theme however was largely cosmetic and under the rear bodywork lurks a traditional 1-litre petrol engine

only the Wankel unit seemed to have enjoyed any form of success. They were only the latest in a long line of oddly configured power units that stretched back to 1900 or so and most were only possible because of the advance in technology.

There was a sudden spurt of activity in this field around 1973, with several designs making an appearance and, in one case, headlines, for the Western Australian government invested $A23,000 in a $A70,000 development programme for a rotary engine designed by an Australian engineer, Ralph Sarich. There was talk of fifteen million dollars worth of backing for the project but by 1978 it seemed as though enthusiasm for the rotary engine had long vanished.

Instead, new types of cylinder head design were improving the efficiency of the conventional reciprocating engine. Even so, manufacturers had little time to experiment, for, especially in America, legislation had fixed many of the design parameters for the power units of the 1980s.

Whether or not the design of the car of the future is markedly different from that of today's vehicles, one thing is sure: the motor vehicle has given man more personal freedom of movement than any other invention.

He will not lightly lay down that freedom at the whim of the politicians. The motor car has covered a long road since the first crude steam and clockwork vehicles made their first appearance; it has a great deal further still to go.

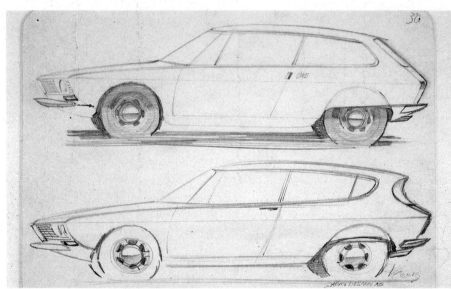

Left and below: Saab design studies; while the engineers struggle manfully to guarantee the future of the motor car beyond the expiry of fossil fuel sources, the industry stylists carry on their own struggle to clothe the engineers' ideas in shapes which will attract the public. The technologists may shape the future, but so long as the public is as fickle as it has been throughout the history of transport, the stylist will shape the car . . .

Chronology 1690-1979

This brief chronology lists, year by year, the milestones in the motoring story, together with photographs of the important cars, so that the speed and scale of development of the motor car can be seen at a glance.

1690 Denis Papin, inventor of the pressure cooker, makes the first proposal for a piston-driven road vehicle.

1769 In Paris, Nicolas Joseph Cugnot makes the first recorded run in a self-propelled steam vehicle, and becomes history's first motor accident, knocking down a wall.

1770 Cugnot builds a larger carriage, still preserved in Paris.

1770 Cugnot steam carriage

1801 The first successful motor vehicle, built by Richard Trevithick, runs through Camborne, Cornwall, but goes up in flames four days later.

1803 Trevithick's second steamer shipped to London, where it makes several successful trips, but frightens the horses and arouses public hostility.

1805 The first-ever internal-combustion engined vehicle built in Switzerland by Isaac de Rivaz. With a foot-operated exhaust valve, it can only run for a few yards.
Oliver Evans puts wheels on his massive steam dredger and drives it through Philadelphia and into the River Schuylkill.

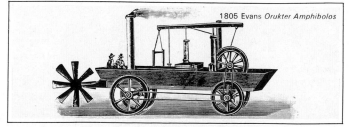

1805 Evans *Orukter Amphibolos*

1816 Reverend Robert Stirling files patents on Stirling engine. Nobody understands why it works.

1829 The first long-distance automobile tour, from London to Bath, made by Goldsworthy Gurney's eighteen-seater, six-wheel steam coach, not without incident.

1830 Walter Hancock's steamer *Infant* begins regular service between Stratford, East London, and Fulham, West London.

1831 British Commission says that steam carriages are practical. Sir Charles Dance operates three Gurney steam carriages between Gloucester and Cheltenham, the world's first scheduled passenger service by automobiles. It lasts only a few months.

1834 Walter Hancock establishes a chain of garages and service stations in London for his passenger-carrying steam omnibuses.

1845 Pneumatic tyres patented by R. W. Thomson of Edinburgh.

1860 J. J. Etienne Lenoir's gas carriage described in *Le Monde Illustré*.

1860 Lenoir gas carriage

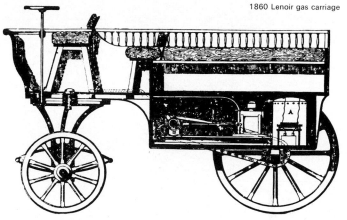

1863 Lenoir's second carriage, with a 1.5hp engine, used for several journeys from Paris to Vincennes – six miles in three hours – running on 'liquid hydrocarbon'.

1864 Lenoir makes history's first export sale of a car, to Alexander II, Tsar of Russia.

1865 'Red Flag Act' passed in Britain; restricts 'Road Locomotives' to 4mph on the open road, 2mph in towns, preceded by a man carrying a red flag (which was not required by law after 1878).

1868 Tangye steamer *Cornubia* exported to India.

1879 George B. Selden files 'master patent' for the automobile in the United States.

1885 Gottlieb Daimler and Wilhelm Maybach convert a horse-carriage to petrol power with a four-stroke engine.

1886 First successful runs of the Benz three-wheeler, the first petrol car to be designed as an entity, not converted from a horse carriage.

1886 Benz

1888 John Boyd Dunlop re-invents the pneumatic tyre.
Magnus Volk begins limited production of electric carriages; one is sold to the Sultan of Morocco.
Karl Benz begins limited production of his three-wheeled cars; but has few orders.

1889 Panhard & Levassor acquire French rights for Daimler's new V-twin engine.

1890 Not being interested in producing cars themselves, Panhard & Levassor grant automotive licence for the Daimler engine to the Peugeot ironmongery business.
Daimler-Motoren-Gesellschaft set up in Cannstatt, Germany.

1890 Panhard & Levassor

1891 M. Levassor changes his mind, and designs and builds a rear-engined car.
Daimler UK rights acquired by Frederick R. Simms, who at first applies the engine solely to motor launches.
French inventor Ferdinand Forest, who in 1885 built an opposed-piston engine with low-tension magneto ignition and a spray carburettor, produces the world's first four-cylinder petrol engine with mechanical valve operation. He will later build the world's first six-cylinder engine, but as both these epoch-making power units were used in boats, not cars, history will tend to ignore him.

1892 Levassor devises the archetypal form of the motor car, with front engine, sliding-gear transmission and rear-wheel drive. It will be known as the *Système Panhard*. In 1893, one of these cars is sold to the Abbé Gavois, a parish priest, who will use it for the next forty years.

1893 The brothers James and Frank Duryea build their motor buggy in Springfield, Massachussetts. Although Lambert, Nadig and Schloemer have all built cars earlier than this, the Duryea is accepted as America's first practicable motor car. However, it is crude compared with the Benz and Daimler vehicles shown at that year's Chicago World Exposition.

1893 Duryea

1894 Benz begins 'mass-production' of the Velo and Viktoria; in 1895, his company will build 135 motor vehicles.
America's first car factory opened by Henry G. Morris and Pedro Salom of Philadelphia to build Electrobat electric cars.
Elwood Haynes and the Apperson brothers collaborate to build an automobile in Kokomo, Indiana.

1894 Benz Viktoria

1894 Benz Velo

1895 Sir David Salomans holds Britain's first motor exhibition at Tunbridge Wells, Kent.
The first indoor exhibition of cars in Britain is held a month later, in November, at the Stanley Cycle Show. One of the five exhibits is the Hon Evelyn Ellis's Panhard, in which the future Edward VII has just had his first petrol-car ride.
After years of revision, Selden's master patent is at last granted in the USA.
De Dion and Bouton produce their first petrol engine.
J. J. Henry Sturmey founds *The Autocar* magazine.
The Lanchester brothers build their first car.
The first car to run on Michelin pneumatic tyres is a Peugeot *L'Eclair*.

1896 Harry J. Lawson launches the Daimler Motor Company in Coventry: the British Motor Industry is born.
Parliament raises the speed limit to 12mph; Lawson organises the Emancipation Day Run from London to Brighton.
American pioneers Henry Ford, Charles Brady King, Ransome Eli Olds and Alexander Winton all complete and test their first cars.
Duryea brings two cars over to Europe for the Emancipation Day event.
Léon Bollée's voiturette is the first car to be sold with pneumatic tyres as standard.
Lawson forms the Great Horseless Carriage Company (later the Motor Manufacturing Company), and seeks to gain control of the British motor industry by acquiring rights to all the vital Continental patents.

1896 Ford

1897 Francis E. and Freelan O. Stanley are the first Americans to produce steam cars commercially.
First large-scale attempt to build cars in America is made by the Pope Manufacturing Company (the country's principal cycle makers) of Hartford, Connecticut.
Sturmey drives a Daimler from John O'Groats to Lands End.
F. R. Simms forms the Automobile Club of Great Britain and Ireland.
First four-cylinder Cannstatt-Daimler ordered by Emil Jellinek.
Death of Emile Levassor.

1898 Stanley

1898 Panhard-Levassor abandon the tiller for wheel steering.
The first De Dion Bouton voiturette appears.
Louis Renault builds his first car, using a De Dion engine and live-axle drive.
Coventry-Daimler's first four-cylinder model appears.
Napier build their first power unit.

1898 Panhard

1898 Daimler four-cylinder

1899 Ransom Eli Olds begins production of the Oldsmobile.
Other companies to begin production this year are: FIAT, Sunbeam, Wolseley, Albion and Isotta-Fraschini.
The first Gardner-Serpollet steam cars appear (Léon Serpollet built his first car in 1887).

1900 The Thousand Miles' Trial, organised by the ACGBI, demonstrates the reliability and efficiency of the motor vehicle to the British public, many of whom had never before seen a car.
Gottleib Daimler dies; a week later the decision is taken to produce the Mercédès, named after Jellinek's teenaged daughter, and designed by Wilhelm Maybach.
American car production totals 4192, sold at an average price of $1000 each.

1901 Mercédès

1901 Lanchester cars go into production.
Cannstatt-Daimler introduces the Mercédès, 'the car of the day after tomorrow' (although none of its technical features is new in itself).

1902 First attempt to drive round the world; but Dr Lehwess's Panhard caravan *Passe Partout* fails to get further than Nijni Novgorod.
Frederick R. Simms founds the Society of Motor Manufacturers and Traders.
The Mercédès-Simplex appears, a vast improvement over the 1901 model.

1902 Mercédès Simplex

1903 Motor Car Act passed in Britain raises speed limit to 20mph, introduces numbering of cars and driving licences (but no test).
First SMMT motor show at the Crystal Palace (London already has two other motor shows, the Cordingley and the Stanley).
Marius Barbarou designs a new front-engined Benz, the Parsifal, to replace the old rear-engined, belt-drive model developed from the 1885–6 prototype.
Henry Ford founds the Ford Motor Company after two earlier attempts to go into car production have failed.
Association of Licenced Automobile Manufacturers formed in America to administer the Selden patent, and sues Ford, among others, for alleged infringement.

331

Spyker of Holland build a six-cylinder, four-wheel-drive racer.
Napier announce the first series-production six-cylinder car.
H. M. Leland founds the Cadillac Motor Car Company in Detroit.
The Vauxhall Iron Works of London build their first car.

1903 Benz Parsifal

1904 Danny Weigel drives a 20hp Talbot 2000 miles non-stop.
Motor Car Act becomes law on New Year's Day.
Ford exports to Britain for the first time.
Mr Rolls meets Mr Royce, and decides to market the Royce car.
Delaunay-Belleville begin production.
Rover, builders of bicycles since the 1880s, begin car manufacture.

1904 Rolls-Royce

1905 Herbert Austin, general manager of Wolseley, resigns to
found his own company at Longbridge, Birmingham.
Automobile Association founded to combat the police 'trapping' of
motorists alleged to have broken the speed limit. Sergeant Jarrett of
Chertsey catches so many motorists that he is promoted to inspector
within the year.

1906 Rolls-Royce Limited floated; the motor trade regards the
capitalisation as a catch-penny scheme.
Ford introduces the $500 Model N; America produces 33,500 cars
in the year.
Racing driver Vincenzo Lancia founds his own company (his father
was a wealthy soup manufacturer).
Adams of Bedford make 60hp Antoinette V8 aero-engine.
Exports of British cars to France total two per month; exports of
French cars to Britain total 400 plus per month.
Charles Glidden of America starts his second round-the-world trip
on his Napier.

332

1907 A 32hp Pilgrim car wins the vapour emission trials organised
by the Automobile Club, which has just been awarded the Royal
accolade by King Edward VII.
Over 60,000 cars are registered in Britain.
Rolls-Royce introduce the 40/50hp six – 'the best car in the world';
under RAC scrutiny, the 40/50 *Silver Ghost* covers 15,000 miles
with only one involuntary stop, at a total cost of £281 8s 4½d, £187
of which was replacement tyres. Forty hours' labour costs comes to
£16 13s 7½d!
A 45hp Hotchkiss also completes a 15,000-mile test, in which it wore
out 46 tyres (value £550).

1907 Pilgrim

1906 Hotchkiss

1908 General Motors Company founded by William Crapo Durant.
Cadillac awarded the Dewar Trophy for standardisation of
production parts.
First Model T Ford built; first year's production totals 8000.

1909 De Dion Bouton introduce their V8, first significant
production model with this engine configuration.
Daimler (GB) adopt the Knight sleeve-valve engine.
Cadillac becomes part of General Motors.

1908 Model T Ford

1910 British Parliament rejects proposal to tax petrol.
Death of the Right Honorable C. S. Rolls in a flying accident at Bournemouth.
Cars are taxed on horsepower ratings devised by the RAC in Britain.
'The New Motoring' craze at its peak, spearheaded by Morgan, GN and Bédélia.
Ettore Bugatti begins production at Molsheim, Alsace (German territory until 1919).
Four-wheel braking offered by Crossley, Arrol-Johnston, Argyll, Isotta-Fraschini.
Experiments made with wireless installation in a car, although the equipment is very bulky.
Sankey pressed-steel detachable wheel introduced.

1917 Cadillac V8

1911 First overseas Ford Factory established at Trafford Park, Manchester; soon becomes Britain's biggest motor manufacturer, with an annual output of 3000 Model Ts.
After protestations that they are not going to abandon the production of steam cars for petrol, the White Company does just this.
Cadillac are the first company to offer electric lighting and starting as standard on their 20/30hp model.
The Selden Patent Case ends with victory for Ford – Selden Patent 'valid but not infringed'.

1912 S. F. Edge resigns from Napier company after a dispute, taking £160,000 'golden handshake' to keep out of the motor industry for seven years. So he turns to pig farming and cattle breeding with great success, and also backs motion-picture production.

1916 Packard Twin-Six

1913 Henry Ford applies the moving conveyor belt to magneto assembly; full assembly-line production comes early the next year, cutting time taken to build a chassis from $12\frac{1}{2}$ to $1\frac{1}{2}$ hours. Sales rise to 182,809.
Cycle and motor agent William Morris, of Oxford, introduces his 10hp Morris-Oxford light car.
Mechanical direction indicators make a tentative appearance.
Lincoln Highway Association formed to lobby for a proper transcontinental road across America.
Fiat build 3251 cars in the year, Renault 9338.

1917 Herbert Austin knighted.
Henry Leland resigns from Cadillac, founds Lincoln Company to build Liberty aero engines.
Chevrolet and General Motors combine.

1918 Car registrations in America exceed five million for the first time.

1919 André Citroën takes over the Mors factory and begins mass-production of his Model A.
Henry Ford buys out all the other stockholders in the Ford Motor Company for $100 million.
Post-war models introduced by Hispano-Suiza, Guy, Enfield-Allday and Bentley all show aero-engine influence in their design.
S. F. Edge takes over AC cars.
Isotta-Fraschini introduce the first production straight-eight.

1913 Morris Oxford 'Bullnose'

1914 Ford workers have their daily pay raised to $5, an industry record.
Over 200 makes of car on the British market.
Renault taxis used to carry French troops to repulse German advance on Paris.

1922 Isotta Fraschini 8

1915 Cadillac announce their V8.
Packard introduce the V12 Twin-Six, inspired by Sunbeam aero-engine designs.
The banker Nicola Romeo takes over the Anonima Lombardo Fabbrica Automobili of Milan, which therefore becomes Alfa Romeo.
Dodge adopt the Budd pressed-steel body.
Everyone who buys a Ford Model T this year gets a $50 rebate because sales have passed their target figure.
Fergus owner-driver car announced.
William Foster & Co of Lincoln build the first successful tank.

1920 This year fifty per cent of all motor vehicles in the world are Model T Fords.
Sudden slump closes many American factories as the post-war market for new cars collapses. Britain's McKenna Duties have put 33.3 per cent tax on imported cars.
Sunbeam, Talbot and Darracq combine to form the STD group, with resultant confusion of badge-engineering, especially among their racing cars.
The Motor-Car Act taxes cars in Britain at £1 per RAC horsepower, crippling sales of the 22hp Model T Ford (but pre-1914 cars pay only half the horsepower rate, and cars used solely for taking

servants to church or voters to the polling station pay no tax at all).
DuPont/Morgan banking interests acquire control of General Motors from Billy Durant; Alfred P. Sloan takes over the running of the group's affairs.
America's first production straight-eight announced by Duesenberg.
Work starts on the Great West Road and Purley Way – Britain's first motor bypasses.
France has 350 car manufacturers.

1920 Model A Duesenberg

1921 Lincoln V8 appears: Henry Ford will take over the company in 1922.
Production of the 3-litre Bentley begins.
Morris cuts prices by up to £100 to boost flagging sales – and doubles his turnover, building 3077 cars in 1921 against 1932 the year before.
Billy Durant borrows $7 million to found Durant Motors.

1922 Lincoln V8

1922 3-litre Bentley

1922 Introduction of the Austin Seven.
Clyno begin car production.
Marconi begin experiments with wireless receivers in Daimler cars.
Over a million Model Ts produced by Ford.
Lancia markets the Lambda, which combines unit body/chassis construction, independent front suspension and V4 engine.
Trico (USA) introduce the electric windscreen wiper – although the vacuum wiper has been around since 1916.
Leyland Motors acquire manufacturing rights to the Trojan.
C. F. Kettering and T. H. Midgley introduce tetraethyl leaded petrol in the USA.

334

1923 Austin Seven

1923 Cecil Kimber builds the first MG, based on his Morris-Cowley sports conversions.
Triumph, famous Coventry cycle manufacturers, build their first car, the 10/20hp.
Ford Model T production peaks at over 2 million.

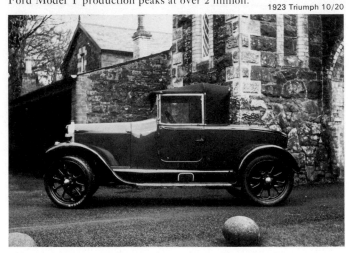

1923 Triumph 10/20

1924 Walter P. Chrysler begins production of the car bearing his name.
DuPont develops quick-drying enamel in the USA, enabling car production to be speeded up.
Napier abandon car production for aero engines.

1924 Chrysler 70

1925 Morris produces 54,151 Bullnose Oxfords and Cowleys.
General Motors acquires Vauxhall Motors of Luton as a European bridgehead.
Ford's British factory produces its 250,000th Model T, which makes a triumphal tour of Britain.
First popular British car with all-round hydraulic braking – the Triumph 13/30.
The Phantom I Rolls-Royce replaces the Silver Ghost, in production since 1906.

1926 In Germany, Benz and Daimler combine to form the Daimler-Benz AG.
The Coventry Daimler Company announces the Double-Six, with a 7136cc V12 sleeve-valve engine.
The General Strike produces London's first commuter traffic jams.
Clyno become the third biggest British motor manufacturer, turning out 300 cars a week in Wolverhampton.
London's first traffic lights.

1927 Model T Ford production ceases after nineteen years and over fifteen million cars. Lowest price during that period – $290 (£65), a record for a conventional motor car.
Wolseley company fails, and is acquired by William Morris.
Chevrolet takes over the top-selling position in the American motor industry as Ford changes over to production of the Model A.
Studebaker and Oldsmobile pioneer the use of chromium plating.
Stanley Steam cars cease production.

1928 Ford Model A

1928 Motor distributors Rootes Limited acquire the Humber and Hillman companies.
Chrysler buys Dodge for $175,000,000.
Clyno attempt to market a £100 version of their new 8hp model – and fail.
Cadillac pioneer synchromesh gearchange.
Alvis produce Britain's first catalogued front-wheel-drive car.

1929 US car production reaches 5,337,087, a peak that will not be exceeded until the 1950s. A total of 26.5 million cars is registered in the USA this year.
Karl Benz dies, aged 85.
Clyno goes into liquidation.
Armstrong-Siddeley fit a Wilson preselector gearbox as an option (standard from 1933) – preselector gears were fitted to the marque's ancestor, the Wilson-Pilcher from 1901–1907.

1930 Sir Dennistoun Burney, highest-paid inventor of World War I, builds the Burney Streamline, with rear engine and all-round independent suspension. Twelve are sold, one to the Prince of Wales.
Daimler fit fluid flywheels in conjunction with preselector gearboxes to produce semi-automatic transmission.
Car sales fall as the Depression deepens.
Henry Royce knighted.
The Veteran Car Club formed to preserve early motor cars – the first organisation of its kind in the world.
British Parliament abolishes the 20mph speed limit (largely ignored by motorists and law enforcers for many years) and introduce compulsory third party insurance.
Cadillac bring out a 7.4-litre V16.
Morris fits hydraulic brakes on his larger production models.

1930 Burney Streamline

1931 Vauxhall introduce syncromesh gears to the British market on the Cadet.
Bentley Motors goes into liquidation. Napier are interested in buying, but are outbid by Rolls-Royce, who form Bentley Motors (1931) Limited.
Daimler acquire Lanchester, Britain's oldest motor manufacturer.
Morris produce a £100 utility two-seat version of the Minor 8hp model.
Ninety per cent of all production cars are now saloons.

1931 Morris Minor

1932 Ford of Britain moves into its new factory at Dagenham on the north bank of the Thames. All plant and machinery moved from Trafford Park over a weekend so no production is lost.
Rootes Group formed.
The first Ford designed specifically for Europe (in Dearborn), the 8hp Model Y, is announced at the Ford Motor Show at London's Albert Hall.
In the USA, Ford introduces the V8, which sells over 300,000 in the first year.

1933 Ford Model Y

1932 Ford V8

1933 William Lyons founds the SS Car Company in Coventry, building luxury coachwork on modified Standard chassis at remarkably low prices.
Semi-automatic transmission offered on Reo cars.
Ford drops into third place in the American automobile industry behind General Motors and the Chrysler Corporation.

1934 Chrysler introduce the revolutionary Airflow line – and overdrive.
British Transport Minister Leslie Hore-Belisha announces a 30mph limit in built-up areas, pedestrian crossings and a driving test.

Morris Motors instal their first moving assembly line at Cowley.
Sir William Morris becomes Baron Nuffield.
Nazis begin building Germany's autobahn system.
Metallic paintwork available on British cars.
Citroën *traction avant* appears; its development is so costly that the company is virtually bankrupted, and André Citroën is forced to sell out to Michelin.

1935 Ford of Britain introduces the first £100 saloon car, a version of the 8hp Model Y.
A world census shows that there are now 35 million motor vehicles in use.
Screenwash system offered by Triumph.
Rootes Group acquires the Sunbeam-Talbot-Darracq combine.

1936 The first Morgan four-wheeler (but still with the 1909-designed independent front suspension).
Fiat introduce the 570cc '500' – nicknamed Topolino (Mickey Mouse) – which, at a UK cost of £120 combines 55mph performance with 55mpg economy.
Porsche builds the first Volkswagens. Hitler, whose Nazi party is financing the development of the VW, will propose that it will be available at a cost of under £50 on an instalment plan.
Britain still has 45 indigenous car manufacturers.
Sir Herbert Austin becomes Baron Austin of Longbridge.
SS Cars introduce their Jaguar model.

1936 Morgan 4/4

1937 SS Jaguar

1937 The SMMT Motor Exhibition is held at Earls Court for the first time, after being at Olympia since 1905.
Germany now has 800 miles of autobahn – at £56,000 a mile.

1938 Britain raises the horsepower tax to £1.25 per hp – and petrol tax from 8d to 9d a gallon.
Standard Flying Eight is the first small British saloon with independent front suspension.
The Nuffield Group takes over Riley.
British manufacturers begin building 'shadow factories' for war production.

1939 Lincoln division of Ford introduces the customised Continental and the lower-priced Mercury.

1940 Car factories in Britain go over to munitions production.
Germans blitz the centre of Coventry.

1941 Death of Lord Austin, aged 74, and of Louis Chevrolet (62).

1943 Due to war production, American passenger car output is cut to just 139 vehicles.

336

1945 Standard acquire Triumph, in liquidation since 1939.
SS cars change their name to Jaguar.
Petrol still rationed in Britain; price now 2s, of which 9d is tax.
Henry Ford II takes over control of the Ford Motor Company from his grandfather, Henry Ford I.
British manufacturers are compelled by the new Socialist government to export half their output. Motorists will have to sign a covenant promising not to sell their new cars for a year, to curb the black market in new vehicles caused by this edict.

1946 British Motor Industry celebrates its fiftieth birthday, and the first post-war British designs, from Armstrong-Siddeley, Triumph, Bentley and Jowett appear.
Petrol ration for British motorists increased 50 per cent.
Ford of Britain produce their millionth car, an 8hp Anglia.

1946 Bentley Mk VI

1946 Ford Anglia 8hp

1947 Golden Jubilee of the American car industry.
Henry Ford dies, aged 84.
Bristol and Frazer-Nash acquire the BMW engine as 'war reparations'.
Ettore Bugatti dies in Paris, aged 66.
Louis Renault, accused of having collaborated with the Germans, is imprisoned and his company nationalised.
David Brown acquires Aston Martin and Lagonda.
Standard Vanguard announced.

1947 Standard Vanguard

1948 First post-war Earls Court Motor Show.
Radical change in British car taxation, which has been based on cubic capacity since the war – henceforward all cars will be taxed at a flat rate, initially £10.
Most notable new cars are the Jaguar XK120, the Issigonis-designed Morris Minor and the Citroën 2CV, originally built before the war, and hidden during the occupation.
American motor industry builds its 100,000,000th car.
Rover launch the four-wheel-drive Land-Rover.

1948 Morris Minor

1949 British petrol restrictions eased; more cars available on the home market.

1950 Ford regains second place in the US industry from Chrysler.
Petrol rationing ends in Britain – but the fuel tax is doubled.
Double purchase tax on luxury cars is halved, although the new-car covenant is extended to two years.
Rover demonstrate the world's first gas-turbine car.
Ford's new Consul and Zephyr models announced.

1951 Lady Docker's first Golden Daimler shown at Earls Court.
Death of Doctor Porsche.
The Triumph TR and the Healey 100 are the first popular-priced sports cars to offer 100mph performance.
Disc braking and power steering are standard items of US Chrysler specification.

1956 Triumph TR

1951 Austin-Healey 100

1952 Austin and Morris companies merge to form the British Motor Corporation, under the chairmanship of Lord Nuffield. Mercédès announce the 300SL sports with 'gull wing' coachwork.

1952 Mercedes 300SL

1953 Branded petrols become available again in Britain; the result is a rise in compression ratios to suit the increased octane ratings. Singer announce the first plastics-bodied British production car, the SMX Roadster.
New-car covenant purchase scheme abolished.

1953 Singer SMX Roadster

1954 General Motors produce its 50 millionth car.
Nash and Hudson combine to form the American Motors Corporation.
Lanchester Sprite is offered with automatic transmission, still a rarity in Europe, although common on American cars.
Volkswagen, having rebuilt their factory after it was gutted in the war, are now well enough established to start a vigorous export drive.
All new American cars are now offered with tubeless tyres.
Ford of America introduce the Thunderbird.

1954 Ford Thunderbird

1955 Citroën introduce the DS19, with hydropneumatic self-levelling suspension, automatic jacks, power steering and braking. The American motor industry's best year yet, with a total production of 9,204,049 vehicles, of which some eight million are passenger cars.

1959 Citroën DS19

1956 Suez crisis cuts supplies of oil to Europe: rationing re-introduced in Britain and other European countries, resulting in a crop of super-economy bubble cars.
American cars begin to sprout tail fins.
Ford Motor Company stock becomes available to the public for the first time when the Ford Foundation offers over ten million shares.
Pininfarina styles BMC cars.
Daimler discontinues production of the Lanchester.

1957 Ford (US) launches the Edsel.
American Motors discontinues the Nash and Hudson marques.
Fiat introduce a new 500, with vertical-twin air-cooled engine and four-speed crash gearbox.
Lotus launch the plastic monocoque-bodied Elite.
Ford build their three millionth Mercury.
Chrysler's ten millionth Plymouth comes off the production line.

1957 Fiat 500 engine

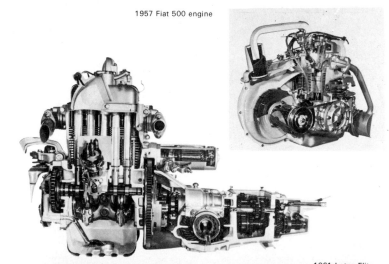

1961 Lotus Elite

1958 Work starts on the M1 Motorway from London to Birmingham, first proposed in 1924.
New 40mph speed limit on roads round London.
Ford celebrates the fiftieth birthday of the Model T by assembling their fifty millionth car (and reassembling a 1909 T).
Chrysler builds its twenty-five millionth vehicle.
Packard builds its last vehicle.
Enter the 'frogeye' Austin-Healey Sprite.
Sir Leonard Lord becomes chairman of BMC.
British manufacturers produce a record one million cars.

1958 Austin-Healey Sprite

1959 Purchase tax on new cars reduced from 60 to 50 per cent.
Lea-Francis go out on a wave of bad taste with the Lynx.
American manufacturers launch their new compact models to combat the growing imports of European small cars.
Alec Issigonis designs the Mini-Minor.
NSU announce that they will build Wankel rotary-engined cars.
Triumph Herald appears, with all-round independent suspension and Michelotti styling.
DAF begin car production, using the Variomatic transmission.

1960 Lea-Francis Lynx

1961 Triumph Herald

1960 Jaguar Cars take over the Daimler Company.
Japanese industry produces 200,000 cars.
Hillman Minx available with Easidrive automatic transmission.
Ford of Britain introduce the 105E Anglia, their first-ever four-speed model, with its raked-back rear window. This car supplanted the ultra-cheap Popular, which still had the 1935 designed 10hp engine and 1938 styling; the 1954 unit-construction Anglia now became the Popular.

1963 Ford Anglia

1961 Transport Minister Ernest Marples introduces testing of all cars over ten years old in Britain.
British car tax raised to £15 from £12 10s a year.
Sir Leonard Lord becomes Lord Lambury.
Morris produce their millionth Minor.
Commercial-vehicle producers Leyland Motors acquire Standard-Triumph and AEC.
Morris 1100 with Hydrolastic suspension introduced.
BMC production reaches 600,000 vehicles a year.
Ford of Britain introduces the Mk I Cortina.

1964 Ford Cortina

1963 The Leyland Motor Corporation formed. Its first chairman, Sir Henry Spurrier, retires through ill-health four months later and dies in 1964.
Death of Lord Nuffield, aged 86.
Hillman's project Ajax is unveiled in the shape of the 875cc Imp, first passenger car to be built in Scotland since the Arrol-Johnston in 1931.
NSU announce the first Wankel car, the Spyder.
Rover announce the 2000 saloon, with a bodyshell inspired by their T4 jet car. It is voted Car of the Year.
Mercedes 600 appears. With a 6.3-litre eight-cylinder engine and an overall length of 20ft 6in, it carries on the tradition of the pre-war *Grosser* Mercedes.

1963 Hillman Imp

1964 Triumph 2000 launched.
Ford of America bring out the Mustang, which sells 500,000 in under 18 months.
Chrysler acquire controlling interest in Rootes.

1964 Triumph 2000

1965 BMC merge with the Pressed Steel Company.
George Harriman, Chairman and Managing Director of BMC is awarded the KBE.
Motor tax increased to £17 10s.
Labour Government brings in blanket speed restriction of 70mph as a 'four-month experiment'.
AP automatic transmission available on the Mini.
Rolls-Royce's first unit-constructed car, the Silver Shadow, is launched.

1966 Jensen launch the four-wheel-drive, 6.3-litre FF.
The Jaguar Group (Jaguar, Daimler, Guy, Coventry, Coventry Climax, Henry Meadows) merges with BMC to form British Motor Holdings.

1966 Jensen FF

1967 Citroën sign an agreement with NSU for joint production of the Wankel engine.
And kill off Panhard, born 1889, which they acquired in 1965 after holding a share in the capital for ten years.
NSU produce the Ro80, first volume-sale Wankel car.
Leyland Motor Corporation acquires Rover and Alvis.
Ford of Europe set up to co-ordinate the production programmes of British and Continental Ford companies.

1973 NSU Ro80

1968 British Motor Holdings merge with Leyland Motors to form the British Leyland Motor Corporation.
Strikes cripple French manufacturers – Renault lose 100,000 units of production.
Volkswagen produce a new model, the 411, alongside the Beetle.

1969 Volkswagen take over Audi.
Jaguar launch the XJ6.

1969 Jaguar XJ6

1970 Range Rover introduced.
GS and SM Citroëns launched.
Ford acquires Ghia of Turin from Alessandro de Tomaso.
Mercedes build the experimental triple-rotor-Wankel C III.
The first water-cooled Volkswagen, the K70, unveiled.
British Leyland launch the five-speed Maxi and drop the Minor.
Chrysler 160/180 range built in France by Simca.
Japan, with a monthly output of 200,000 cars, is now the world's second biggest motor manufacturer.

1970 Citroen GS

1971 Jensen drops the FF and is taken over by Norwegian-born, American-based Kjell Qvale.
Ralph Nader, having crucified the Chevrolet Corvair in his 1965 book *Unsafe at any Speed*, turns his attention to the VW Beetle.
Aston Martin, in financial difficulties, is sold by the David Brown Group to financiers who continue production of the DBS.
Jaguar V12 revealed.
Aero-engine division of Rolls-Royce goes into liquidation.

1972 British motor industry produces 1,900,000 cars in this year.
Datsun becomes the second biggest importer of cars into Britain.

1973 The Arab–Israeli War causes oil supply restrictions and threats of petrol rationing.
50mph speed limit imposed in Britain until fuel supplies are stabilised.
Ford opens automatic transmission plant in Bordeaux.
Volkswagen beat the Model T's production record with the Beetle.
British motorists queue for petrol.

1974 Peugeot take over Citroën.
E. L. Cord and Gabriel Voisin die.
Fiat run into grave financial problems.
General Motors cancel plans to build 100,000 Wankel-engined Vegas.
American manufacturers veer away from large-engined cars in search of fuel economy. Dealers have a record 80 days' stock of unsold cars.
Ford begin research into highly efficient Stirling 'hot-air' engine.
Fiat build a million 127s.
Volkswagen introduce contemporary styled Golf models.

1974 Alfasud

1975 Rolls-Royce unveil the Camargue, priced at £31,000.
Porsche Carrera Turbo, is announced.
Chrysler-UK in financial difficulties, but saved by public finance.
Chrysler's French-produced Alpine brings much needed business.
Volvo gains a majority shareholding in the DAF company.
Volvo, Peugeot and Renault flagships use a communal V6 motor.
Citroën's CX, Car of the Year, replaces the DS range.
£200 million injected into strike-hit British Leyland, giving National Enterprise Board a 95% stake in the company.
Jaguar sports cars ousted as the E-type is superseded by the XJS.
Lotus' supercar image consolidated with Esprit and Eclat models.

1976 Chrysler Alpine voted Car of the Year.
Rover's stylish 3500 introduced.
Audi-NSU experiment with a Wankel engine in the Audi 100.
Ford's first front-drive car, the Fiesta, announced.

1976 Porsche Turbo

1977 Michael Edwardes inherits Leyland's many problems.
Volkswagen drop the Beetle (except in South America) after a forty-year run.
Panther show '200 mph' six-wheeler at Britain's *Motorfair*.
Stop-go wedding between Saab and Volvo finally called off.
NSU call it a day with the rotary-engined Ro80.
Porsche introduce water-cooled, front-engined 924 and 928 models.
928 voted Car of the Year

1978 Dutch Government props up ailing Volvo-DAF operation with £18½ million financial aid.
Michael Edwardes' tough approach reaps impressive results at Leyland but the company's future remains in the balance.
Mazda keep faith with the rotary engine and introduce the widely acclaimed RX-7 sports coupé.
Volkswagen introduce impressive diesel-engined Golf.

Index

Page numbers in roman type indicate that an entry is mentioned in the text on those pages, whereas italic page numbers indicate that an entry appears in a caption

344